M000111642

SPORTS CAR COLOR

JAGUAR

E-TYPE

Matthew L. Stone

Motorbooks International
Publishers & Wholesalers ®

First published in 1995 by Motorbooks International
Publishers & Wholesalers, 729 Prospect Avenue,
PO Box 1, Osceola, WI 54020-0001 USA

Motorbooks International is a certified trademark,
registered with the United States Patent Office

The information in this book is true and complete to
the best of our knowledge. All recommendations are
made without any guarantee on the part of the
author or Publisher, who also disclaim any liability
incurred in connection with the use of this data or
specific details

We recognize that some words, model names and
designations, for example, mentioned herein are the
property of the trademark holder. We use them for
identification purposes only. This is not an official
publication

Motorbooks International books are also available at
discounts in bulk quantity for industrial or sales-
promotional use. For details write to Special Sales
Manager at the Publisher's address

Library of Congress Cataloging-in-Publication Data
Stone, Matthew L.
    Jaguar E-type / Matthew L. Stone.
        p.   cm. — (Sports car color history)
    Includes index.
    ISBN 0-7603-0071-2 (pbk.)
    1. Jaguar E-type automobile—History. I. Title.
    II. Series.
TL215.J3S76 1995
629.222'2—dc20   95-393

On the front cover: John and Linda Phillips' concours-
winning 1973 Series III V-12 roadster. Location courtesy
of the Deer Creek Winery in Escondido, California. *David
Newhardt*

On the frontispiece: Designer and artist Gene Garfinkle,
IDSA, captures the early 1960s look and feel of the
quintessential E-Type, a Series I 3.8 roadster. This work,
which is new and previously unpublished, is done in
Prismacolor on canson paper in a style reminiscent of that
used in design studios of the era.

On the back cover: Top: Jose Otero's 1963 Series I 3.8
coupe among the hills of California's legendary Angeles
Crest Highway. Is there a more classic car and paint
combination than that of E-Type and British Racing Green?
David Newhardt **Bottom:** The E-Type's American debut at
the New York Auto Show, 1961.

Printed in Hong Kong

CONTENTS

Introduction and Acknowledgments

My passion for Jaguar's E-Type was most likely ignited at precisely the same moment as yours: the first time I ever saw one.

I don't remember where or when it was, but as early as my affection for automobiles began to fester, I was acutely aware of the E-Type. That shape, captivating then as now, with those unbelievably sporty wire wheels; automotive overload for a ten year old far more enamored with Mario Andretti than Sandy Kolfax. I got my driver's license at 8:31 A.M. on my sixteenth birthday, and thought something like a black E-Type roadster would be the perfect first car for a leadfooted teenager; my ever-pragmatic dad thought otherwise. He's a car buff of the first order, but thought something a bit more "practical" (translation: something not so bloody fast) would be a better choice. He said E-Types spent most of their time parked by the side of the road, either getting a ticket (the red ones) or broken down (any color will do).

I can't tell you how many E-Types he talked me out of: that black '68 roadster or pristine white '74 V-12 roadster available with 8,000 original miles on it, for only 8,000 original dollars. On the flip side, he also talked me out of a '71 V-12 coupe that had too much Bondo in it to ever rust and a maroon '72 sounded much like the solid lifters in a Top Fuel dragster with a dry crankcase. What I am of course getting around to is that he definitely "knew a good one from a bad one."

As they say, "when it's right, you'll know it," and one particular Willow Green 1967 E-Type was oh so right. I purchased "R P SOUP" from car club friends Alan and LaVonne Epstein; Alan bought the car brand new as a birthday present for LaVonne in late 1966. Thus I was only the second owner. What sort of shape was it in, you ask? I remember sheepishly querying Alan as to whether the car had any rust in it. A standard E-Type type question, right? His eyes sharpened, and his voice deepened measurably as he assured me that "this car has never spent a night out in the *dew*." Enough said.

I have been fortunate enough to own two other examples of Sir William's craft: a somewhat tatty 1964 3.8 S sedan (excuse me, *saloon*) and a portly but equally charming 1967 420 G. Each owes a bit of its heritage to the E-Type, and I enjoyed them both as well. More Jaguars are likely to be a part of my future.

It may not be good form to begin making apologies for this book before you so much as venture into the first chapter, but there is one disclaimer I must offer: this book, as no other before or since, could even represent an attempt at the all-encompassing E-Type saga. Philip Porter's *Jaguar E-Type: The Definitive History* makes a credible effort to do so, but the point is this: the story is simply too large and too deep for any one volume to cover. For the true history buff, the car's design and development could fill a book of its own. We will chart the major changes during the car's thirteen-year production life, though you won't find comments like "diameter of oil pump shaft increased by 1 mm beginning with chassis number so-and-so." E-Type racing lore could (and *should*) be the subject of a another major work, given the fantastic body of archival photographs that exists. There are several volumes strictly dedicated to restoration. And so on. What we *have* attempted to do is bring you a worthwhile look at the E-Type's upbringing, plus some exciting new photography showing off the car's legendary appearance. Advertising and sales brochure art bring additional period focus to the story. Some of the sidebar topics are "on the lighter side," and the book generally deals with the car from an American market and model perspective.

A word about nomenclature: you'll see this model described alternately as an "E" Type, an XK-E, an E-Type, an XKE, etc. Various versions have been used, even in Jaguar's own advertising. For consistency's sake, we'll use what many consider to be the most proper version, the "E-Type."

Like the Academy Award Winner with a case of flap-jaw, I'd like to thank the following folks for their involvement in, or influence upon, this book:

I thank the aforementioned father, Milt Stone,

for teaching me young and teaching me well about automobiles, and about *life,* for that matter. The above kidding far aside, he gave much more good advice than bad. Condolences to my mother Bella for putting up with all this car rubbish for so many years, and for having to drive a '58 Austin Healey even though she was eight months pregnant. Apologies to my sister Marla, who had to forsake Barbies and normal girl-type things for learning how to wax paint and change oil; she is converting brother-in-law Eric to a car guy too.

Deepest thanks to my wife Linda, as this work assuredly took time away from other things. She steadfastly encouraged me to pursue a writing career years ago, and does a marvelous job of proofreading copy she doesn't begin—or pretend—to understand! Much love to my twin daughters Maureen and Melissa, who always relished a ride in Daddy's Green Car.

I can't even calculate my appreciation for the support given me by journalist peers such as the late Dean Batchelor, Rob de la Rive Box, Greg Brown, Cynthia Claes, John M. Clor, Matt DeLorenzo, Len Frank, Jim Sawyer, Kevin Wilson, Tom Wilson, and all my friends of the Motor Press Guild. Each of these folks patiently mentored this rookie scribe in one way or another when I was making my start in this business.

Extra thanks to David W. Newhardt, the talented shooter who captured many of the photographs contained herein. Even if you haven't seen his work before, trust me when I say you'll be seeing a lot more of it in the future. Other contributing photographers included Bob Tronolone, Bob Dunsmore, and Scott Mead. Their work is identified in captions throughout the book.

Many car owners were kind enough to pose their prized machines for our cameras, and they are: Mr. and Mrs. Ron Cressey, 1963 Series I Roadster; Mr. and Mrs. George Lassus, 1967 Series I Coupe; Mr. Jose Otero, 1963 Series I Coupe; Mr. and Mrs. John Phillips, 1973 Series III Roadster; Mr. and Mrs. Hank Spires, 1971 Series III Coupe; Mr. and Mrs. Jim Belardi, 1967 Series I Coupe; Mr. and Mrs. Pat Barry, 1967 Series I 2+2; Mr. and Mrs. Bob Curry, 1969 Series II Roadster.

Thanks as well to those whose cars may have been "snapped" somewhere along the way, but whose names are unknown to us.

This book did not go from my cameras and computer to the printed volume you hold in your hand without a lot of help and support from the folks at Motorbooks Publishing, most particularly my editor Zack Miller. Zack patiently answered my every question, and believe me, there were a bunch. He encouraged and fostered creativity, and was always open-minded about new ideas. A down-to-earth, yet completely professional individual.

This project would have surely been stillborn had it not been for the assistance and support provided by Jaguar Cars, Inc., and especially the following personnel: Michael Dale, President, Jaguar Cars, Inc.; Mark Miller, Vice President, Public Affairs, Jaguar Cars, Inc.; Eileen Devlin, Public Affairs, Jaguar Cars, Inc.; Karen Miller, Archivist, Jaguar Cars Archives (USA); Ann Harris, Archivist, Jaguar Daimler Heritage Trust (UK).

It's inspiring to see how enthusiastically Jaguar recognizes and supports its heritage, as well as the people who harbor such feelings for its products. Ms. Miller and Ms. Harris provided a considerable amount of the archival photography for this work, and without their help and research, finding artwork for this project would have been akin to going on an archeological dig. Ms. Miller was especially kind in responding to my many faxes, voice mail, and phone calls!

Additionally, I acknowledge the following folks and firms who have, in one way or another, contributed: Jaguar Clubs of North America (JCNA); John Radovich, John's Cars; Bob Tullius, Group 44; Brian Lister; Lou Fidanza, Gran Turisimo Jaguar; Bernard Juchli; Ron Greim; Mark Mayuga; Jeff Herbert; Kathy Johnson, Aston Martin Lagonda of North America; Patrick Paternie, another up-and-coming journalist who authored two of the sidebar topics in this book; Gene Garfinkle, friend, gifted designer, and artist who created the original artwork found on the frontis; and Mike, Jean, and Jeff O'Brien, along with the rest of the gang at Flags Photo Center of Pasadena, California.

Lastly, my thanks to *you,* the reader. You reached into your pocket, extracted your hard-earned cash (or your hard-earned credit card), and bought this book. Were it not for you, I would not have had the opportunity to write. I appreciate your gesture, and I sincerely hope you enjoy *Jaguar E-Type.*

—Best Regards, Matthew L. Stone 1995

JAGUAR
1

*In order to gain a clear vision of where
one is about to go in life, one must first gain
an understanding of where it is one has been,
and whether or not it was a worthwhile trip.*
—Anonymous

Before the E

The E-Type didn't just "happen." For all its new-
ness and impact when introduced, the car's lineage is relatively simple to trace. From a purely
historical standpoint, the E-Type's ancestral
progenitor would likely be the SS 100. Undeniably one of the premier prewar sporting
machines, the 100 is one of the cars that put Sir
William Lyons' fledgling concern on the map.
However, the real design and mechanical foundation for the E-Type was cast just after World War
II. The year was 1948, the car the XK 120.

XK 120

Its amusing to note that one of Jaguar's most
beloved sports car models really was the byprod-
uct of "sedan car" development. In short, the XK
120 was almost an afterthought, initially a show-
stopping engine stand in which to display Jaguar's
new six-cylinder engine. The real target for the
new powerplant was the Mark VII sedan, which
was to be Jaguar's first new product after WW II.
The 2.5 and 3.5 ltr OHV sixes had served well, but
were now quite long in tooth, both being essentially products of the thirties. Jaguar's Chief Engineer, William Heynes, along with company cre-
ator and patriarch William Lyons (see sidebar)

**Like D-Types, C-Types are also quite popular in historic
racing circles, such as this example, running at the 1991
Monterey Historic Auto Races.** *Bob Dunsmore photo*

The intended first recipient of the new XK engine, the Jaguar Mk VII sedan. Don't let the size and classically curvaceous styling fool you: these cars were capable of a genuine 100 mph cruising speed in production form and saw more than their fair share of racetrack time.

The first true Sport Sedan? As an interesting aside, this 1952 model still belongs to its original owner, Sam Anslyn of Northridge, California. As of this writing, Anslyn owns five other Jaguars. *Author photo*

started virtually from scratch, developing an all-new six-cylinder powerplant employing design architecture and materials heretofore seen exclusively in race-only applications or the most elite luxury performance cars. Actually, four-, six-, and even twelve-cylinder designs were initially conceived, though the latter fell by the wayside early. The four-cylinder lived to prototype stage, and a handful of cars carried it (dubbed the "XK-100"), but the six handily met management's development criteria, surviving to become the staple of Jaguar's powerplant line-up for nearly forty years.

If there was any feature of the XK six that put it on the map, it was the use of an alloy head featuring twin overhead cams (DOHC). Involved in its development was Harry Weslake, who by the end of the war had developed quite a reputation as an expert on cylinder heads and combustion chamber design. Also a key figure in all postwar Jaguar engine development was an engineer named Walter Hassan, who would figure heavily in

the later V-12 projects. Weslake and Heynes came up with a cross-flow design featuring hemispheric combustion chambers, placing the spark plug in the "dome" portion of the chamber to promote efficient combustion. As noted, the head was produced in weight-saving aluminum, mounted to an iron block. The block carried a seven-bearing crankshaft, fully counterweighted, and employed wet-sump oiling, though many a racing model would later employ a dry sump and tank.

The camshafts were driven by a set of two chains, the valves placed at an angle of 70 degrees. The engine was considered a 3.4 ltr (actually 3442 cc), translating to approximately 210 ci. Carburetion for that first XK was via dual 1-3/4-in sidedraft SU carburetors. With a compression ratio of 8.0:1, the engine was rated at 160 hp at 5400 rpm. To put this engine's impact and capability into focus, the V-8 engine found in most Fords of the day was all-iron, used a single carburetor and a valve-in-head design, and put out about 100 hp. The 2.6-ltr six found in the Aston Martin DB 2 put out a mere 107 bhp. This powerplant was assuredly the stuff of which legends would be—and were—made.

As noted, the XK engine development program was really targeted at the Mk VII sedan range, though as this new car was not quite production-ready at the time, Lyons and Company elected to show the engine off in a prototype sports roadster (this statement is misleading in a sense, however, as the Mk VII chassis really had been completed, but was offered with its predecessor's coachwork and pushrod engines). This interim model was dubbed the "Mk V."

As the XK engine project neared completion in 1948, it came to Lyons that perhaps a worthy successor to the SS 100 was feasible. According

What better way to display a manufacturer's new engine than in a shape such as the XK 120's? This original XK roadster, replete with split windshield and fender skirts, is considered by many to be among the purest automotive shapes ever contrived. It's certainly among the best ever actually *built. Jaguar Daimler Heritage Trust*

The Whitehead/Walker XK 120C leads a pair of Chrysler-powered Cunninghams shortly after the start of the 1951 24 Hours of Le Mans, Jaguar's first win at the Sarthe circuit. To the right is an Aston Martin and, just behind, a Jaguar XK 120 licensed for the street. *Jaguar Archives*

The D-Type's first win at the Rheims twelve-hour event in 1954. Given the success of the C-Type, the D-Type had big shoes to fill. Not to worry, as it would go on to win (among others) the 24 Hours of Le Mans three times straight, and it was, of course, an obvious precursor to the E-Type. This Whitehead/Wharton-driven D-Type was entered by the Jaguar factory. *Jaguar Archives*

to Lyons, "such a car with the XK engine could not fail, provided of course we made no serious mistake, to become outstanding, as it should easily out perform everything else on the market by a wide margin, irrespective of price." As a result, a Mk V chassis was shortened from its 120 inch wheelbase to 102 inches, and it employed what would essentially be the Mk VII suspension.

Attached to the chassis was the curvaceous and simply stunning coachwork, rendered in aluminum for the show car, several of the first prototypes, and early production cars. Designed inhouse, and primarily inspired by William Lyons (as were virtually all Jaguars of the 1950s and 1960s), the look was a refreshing hint at where postwar sports car design was headed. Amazingly, the design of the body shell was done in less than a month's time. The 3.4-ltr XK was backed by a four-speed transmission; the car was dubbed "XK 120" owing to both the name of the revolutionary new engine and its theoretical top speed potential of 120 mph.

The Motor commented that "the open two seater has become a thing of sweeping curves and enclosing metal." *Road & Track* would later note that "the car has a rather awkward appearance with its far-from-weatherproof top in place,

and looks even more homely with the fender skirts installed but, in spite of these points, we predict that the styling and performance of the Jaguar XK 120 will bring it immediate and lasting success in the U.S. Market." Damnation by faint praise? No fear: the XK 120 "stole" the 1948 British Motor Show at Earls Court. Jaguar had a fistful of orders, and the production XK 120 became a reality.

As noted, Jaguar built the earliest alloy-bodied 120s in-house from late 1949 through mid-1950; from then on, coachwork was stamped out by the Pressed Steel panel company in steel on permanent tooling. Did the XK 120 really live up to its advance billing? Absolutely. As a bit of a public relations event, Lyons and Bill Heynes flew a group of journalists and other hangers-on to Belgium in May of 1949 for a trial. Test driver Ron Sutton drove a stock, alloy-bodied 120 down the Jabbeke highway at a mean average speed of 126.448 mph. Subsequent tests with different cowling, windshields, etc., yielded even higher numbers; it was clear that "XK 120" was no misnomer.

Road & Track's prognostication of success in the U.S. was quite accurate. The car premiered in America at the 1950 New York Motor Show, and was no less a sensation there than it was in England a few shows before. Available as a pure roadster, a drop-head coupe, or a "fixed-head coupe," the XK 120 came to these shores and was greeted by postwar, performance-starved arms. The XK 120, along with the MG TD and TC models, effectively introduced postwar America to the pleasures and perils of sports car motoring. These sporting Jaguars also achieved notable success in American sports car racing; many great American drivers, such as Dan Gurney and Phil Hill, cut their teeth on modified 120s.

The various XK 120 models were produced through September of 1954, when a revised design, the XK 140, was introduced. The XK 140 featured a host of performance and reliability upgrades. The standard 3.4-ltr XK was now rated at 190 hp, equaling the output of "special equipment" engines available in the XK 120. SE-engined 140s were now rated at 210 hp—again at a time when Ford's newest OHV V-8 was putting

out 50 hp less! In late 1956, an automatic transmission available on FHC and DHC models, perhaps to compete with the automotics available on the new Ford Thunderbird and Chevrolet Corvette? The XK 140 was manufactured through February of 1957.

The last model in the XK trilogy is the XK 150. The XK 150 is a significant element in the E-Type story for at least two reasons: one, it was the model that directly predated the E-Type in Jaguar's line-up; and two, in 3.8/-ltr "S" trim, it carried three carburetors and was rated at 265 hp—the engine that, with very little refitting, would power the first series E-Types. The XK 150 was substantially restyled, the doors no longer having the deep, curving "cut down" seen on the original 120. The grille shape and size was changed, the interior trimmed more luxuriously, and rack and pinion steering was added.

For what began life as essentially a prototype "dream car," the XK series lived an approx-

If ever a machine deserved the phrase "thinly disguised race car," the XK-SS is it. It's D-Type all the way, and the minimal interior accommodations, deck-mounted luggage rack, and minuscule exhaust systems do little to mask the XK's race track heritage. It's now one of the most sought after Jaguar models. *Jaguar Archives*

Sir William Lyons

It wasn't so long ago that entire car companies were the vision of but one man. Ferrari is now owned by Fiat, Lamborghini by MegaTech, and, of course, Jaguar is a part of the Ford stable. But from early in its history until the formation of the British Leyland Motor Corporation in 1968, Jaguar was "driven" almost exclusively by Sir William Lyons.

Born September 4, 1901, Lyons was headlong into the manufacturing business by age twenty-one. He was co-founder of the Swallow Sidecar Company, which manufactured motorcycle sidecars. The business grew quickly and soon included the production of special bodies—called "Swallow"—on proprietary chassis, the most popular being the Austin 7.

William Lyons in Blackpool, England, circa 1922. A good portion of Swallow's early business was in making motorcycle sidecars. Interestingly enough, the dapper Lyons was not aboard a British-built bike, but an American Harley-Davidson! *Jaguar Daimler Heritage Trust*

Lyons entered the ranks of automobile manufacturers in 1931 with the introduction of his own car, the SS1, which was an immediate sensation. There followed, in rather rapid succession, a stream of extremely successful models, including the SS Jaguar sedans and the SS 100 sports cars, to name but two. The sidecar business was ultimately sold off, and the automotive interest was renamed "Jaguar Cars."

Though WW II interrupted production and growth, Lyons pushed aggressively for new engine, chassis, and body designs immediately after the war. Sir William (he was knighted in 1956) continued to manage virtually every aspect of the company through the heydays of the 1950s and early 1960s, acquiring several other firms along the way: Daimler, Guy Motors, Henry Meadows Ltd., and Coventry Climax (famous for racing engines).

In 1968, he joined forces with Sir George Harriman of BMC, announcing a joint venture called "BMH" (British Motor Holdings). Leyland soon joined the fold, the ultimate result being British Leyland. Sir William Lyons retired from full-time service at Jaguar in 1972. But he stayed in touch with the company he founded, especially in the early 1980s, when Jaguar broke away from British Leyland (in 1984) and came under the stewardship of John Egan. Egan was said to have consulted with Lyons quite regularly, helping the firm prosper in its post-Leyland independence.

There is much to be said about William Lyons the man, but as a car builder he seemed to be able to imbue his products with at least two unique attributes: quality far exceeding their cost; and a truly elegant style. The first stemmed from Lyons' firm belief in offering better "value for money" than the competition. While Jaguars were certainly not inexpensive cars, they generally possessed the styling, features, technological advancements, and performance of cars costing 20–50 percent more. As for the second, while others, particularly stylist/aerodynamicist Malcolm Sayer, had

An older and statelier now-*Sir* William Lyons in front of his country home, Wappenbury Hall, in Warwickshire, England. The car is a Series II 4.2 coupe in Willow Green, said to be one of Sir William's preferred colors. *Jaguar Daimler Heritage Trust*

influence on the look of Jaguar's models, the main inspiration for their handsomely feline character was definitely Sir William's. Fans and detractors alike will testify to his sense of style, line, and proportion.

There are many and varying opinions about Lyons: he was kind, he was mercurial; he was sensible, he was cheap; he was honest, he was ruthless. In truth, he was probably all of that and more, and while Managing Director Lofty England, Chief of Engineering Bill Heynes, Malcolm Sayer, Walter Hassan, Claude Bailey, Phil Weaver, Harry Weslake, Norman Dewis, and dozens more certainly were instrumental in the history of Jaguar, there's little doubt that Sir William Lyons *was* Jaguar for the nearly fifty years he ran the company. He passed away in February 1985, at age eighty three.

imately twelve-year production life, and was not only a mainstay of Jaguar's sporting line-up throughout the 1950s, but spawned several race models that would rewrite racing record books throughout the same decade. They remain exceptionally popular sports cars in any circles.

XK 120C

Often later referred to as the C-Type (for competition), the XK 120C was Jaguar's first postwar, purpose-built racing model. Several privateers entered nearly stock XK 120s for the 1950 running of the 24 Hours of LeMans and did surprisingly well, one entry running as high as third prior to retiring. Lyons commissioned Bill Heynes and his development team to construct works-sponsored cars for the 1951 event.

The C-Type's handsome bodywork design was smaller, lighter, and more aerodynamic than that of the standard XK 120; it was the work of Malcom Sayer (see sidebar), whose talent would affect the shape of Jaguars for decades to come. The chassis was a well-triangulated tubular affair, upon which the alloy coachwork was mounted in such a way that it could be easily removed for pit repairs. The cockpit was "business only," also paneled in aluminum, and held little more than two small seats, gauges, and a small, cut-down windshield.

The XK powerplant received the usual race prep at the charge of Harry Weslake: careful assembly, larger valves, port enlargement, higher lift camshafts, etc. The result was an estimated 200–210 hp. More was possible, but the goal was performance along with twenty-four-hour durability. A larger-than-stock clutch was employed along with a slightly modified four-speed transmission and a Salisbury rear differential, but the overall mechanical specification was straightforward and remarkably similar to that of a stock XK 120.

The C's recipe of lighter weight, more aerodynamic shape, and increased horsepower delivered substantial performance gains, and appeared more than a match for the competition at LeMans. *Road & Track* tested one in 1951 (which belonged to Masten Gregory) and achieved a 0–60 mph time of 6.6 sec, 0–100 mph time of 16.8 sec, and a top speed of 141 mph. This test was conducted using a 3.92 final drive ratio; with the C-Type's more commonly used 3.31 rear gear, top speed was well above 150 mph.

Jaguar allowed Briggs Cunningham to enter the E2A prototype in selected races, including Le Mans. It's shown here in the hands of future three-time World Driving champion Jack Brabham at the now-defunct Riverside International Raceway on October 17, 1960 (note the car's race number), competing in the Los Angeles Times Gran Prix (though it failed to finish). *Bob Tronolone photo*

Three works C-Types were entered at LeMans for 1951, and the factory roster of drivers included soon-to-be-Gran Prix legend Stirling Moss. To say they were successful would be a remarkable understatement. At the four-hour mark, it was Jaguar running 1–2–3! Unfortunately, the Moss-Fairman car broke a connecting rod, and the Johnson-Biondetti machine lost oil pressure. In contrast, the C-Type of Peter Whitehead and Peter Walker built up a substantial lead and survived to give Jaguar its first outright victory at LeMans, not to mention the first for a British team since 1935.

The 1952 race went to Mercedes, but Jaguar was back with a full contingent for 1953. The results were even more convincing than the '51 effort: Duncan Hamilton and Tony Rolt brought C-Type #18 home first overall, with Peter Walker and Stirling Moss crossing the line in second. Nineteen-fifty-one co-winner Peter Whitehead joined Ian Stewart in yet another XK 120C, coming home fourth, giving Jaguar a 1–2–4 finish. The C-Type would race successfully in Europe and the United States, but its accomplishment of two overall LeMans victories in three years assured it a place as one of Jaguar's most significant competition models—and the one that made Jaguar a force to be reckoned with in international sports car racing.

D-Type

As good as the C-Type was, increasing competition from Mercedes and relative newcomer

Ferrari forced Jaguar management to respond with an even more potent competition model. Lyons, Sayer, and Heynes, still employing the XK engine as a foundation, developed the now-legendary D-Type.

The D-Type differed from the C-Type in several ways. While the C-Type was strictly a tube frame design, the D-Type employed stressed panels in a monocoque configuration aft of the firewall, along with space frame construction in the engine compartment area. The C-Type's drum brakes were never more than adequate, so the D-Type mounted disc brakes at all corners. The engine was tuned to high specifications and employed a full dry-sump lubrication system for greater reliability. With sharper cam timing than the C-Type and an intake system now comprised of three sidedraft Weber carburetors, output was between 250 and 290 hp, depending upon the specifics of each car. Dunlop alloy disk wheels replaced the C-Type's alloy wires.

Malcom Sayer designed an all-time classic shape for the new racer: purposeful yet graceful, its alloy skin stretched so tightly over the mechanicals it fairly pinged when you touched it. The most mysterious touch was the optional stabilizing fin that attached to the driver's headrest. Hints of the production E-Type—still more than five years away—were already visible. The passenger area received a removable alloy cover to further aid aerodynamics.

If the C-Type was successful, the D-Type was all-conquering. Looking again at LeMans for example, the D-Type picked up just about where the C-Type left off. While Ferrari narrowly beat the D-Type in its first appearance, winning the 1954 event, Jaguar was back in 1955, winning that tragedy-marred event (a Mercedes driven by Pierre Levegh went into the crowd, killing the driver and more than eighty spectators). Winners Mike Hawthorn and Ivor Bueb battled with the Mercedes team, particularly the 300 SLR driven by Juan Manuel Fangio, until the Mercedes team withdrew from the event after the accident. Aston Martin came home second, with the John Claes/Jacques Swaters D-Type in third.

It would be difficult to discuss D-Type racing history without mentioning Ecurie Ecosse, the Scottish run team that dominated this era of European sports car racing as convincingly as, say,

Team Cunningham D-Type, as shown on a gift shop postcard, photographed outside the original Briggs Cunningham Automotive Museum in Costa Mesa, California. Cunningham himself competed in this particular car. *Author collection*

Team Penske has recently done in IndyCar. The deep-blue racing machines and multi-car transporter are a fixture in many photographs taken trackside. Ron Flockhart and Ninian Sanderson beat a commanding roster of Gran Prix stars in an Ecurie Ecosse D-type to win Jaguar's fourth LeMans in 1956: Stirling Moss and Peter Collins brought an Aston Martin DB3S in second, with Maurice Trintignant and Olivier Gendebien taking third in a Ferrari 625 LM. The Swaters/Rouselle D-type finished fourth, with '55 winners Hawthorn and Bueb managing sixth in yet another D-Type.

Though the term "threepeat" had yet to be coined, Jaguar pulled off what was thought virtually impossible by winning the 1957 24 Hours of LeMans in convincing fashion. Prior winners Ivor Bueb and Ron Flockhart brought their Ecurie Ecosse D-Type home first, with teammates Ninian Sanderson and Jack Lawrence in second. Other independent teams placed third, fourth, and sixth in other D-Types. Five of the top six places for 1957, three wins in a row for the D-Type, and five wins in a single decade for Jaguar! And this record only covers one event.

In America one of the most notable D-Type entrants was Briggs Cunningham. Cunningham had since quit building his own cars, and ran D-Types with great results around the country, but by 1958 the car's day was coming to an end: European regulations restricted the D-Type to only 3.0 ltr, and the V-8- and V-12-powered

Maseratis and Ferraris were beginning to exercise their dominance. The D-Type's live axle was also not able to deliver quite the handling of some of the newer machinery with IRS. Still, the D-Type represents a high-water mark for Jaguar as perhaps its most successful competition model.

XK-SS

If ever a car deserved the moniker "thinly disguised race car," the XX-SS is it. Other than several prototypes that would follow, the so-called street XK-SS also represents the truest hint of the E-Type sports car to come a few years later. The initial rush of privateer purchases had subsided, and with competition advancing and rules changing, Jaguar found itself with too many unsold units by the end of 1956 (which was, in a way, a bit surprising, as Jaguar's biggest win at LeMans would come six months later!). Jaguar announced its withdrawal from direct involve-

In January of 1957, Jaguar's management made the decision to convert the remaining cars to street specification, an ultra-high-performance alternative to the production XK 140s. The United States would be the car's intended market. The job was fairly simple, and largely cosmetic. A minuscule passenger door was added, as were a wraparound windshield, side windows, and a folding top. Due to the virtually nonexistent luggage space, a chrome luggage rack was added to the deck, and slim bumpers (not unlike those that would appear on the Series I E-Type) sprouted from the fenders. A minimal exhaust system did little to calm the racing spec 3.4 XK's bark; a few road lamps were added; and presto, the D-Type became the XK-SS. The balance of the D-Type's racing hardware was left intact, including the pin drive Dunlop wheels, 38-gal fuel tank, sidedraft Webers, and dry-sump oiling system. The engine was not detuned in any noticeable way, and the XK-SS was even delivered wearing racing tires!

Road & Track tested two XK-SSs and commented that "as a thinly disguised road-racing machine it will delight the enthusiast. On the other hand, anyone contemplating buying the SS for the purpose of driving it to and from the office and running in a occasional rally would be well advised to forget it." *R & T* recorded a best 0–60 mph time of 4.2 sec, a best standing quarter mile time of 13.8 sec, and a top speed nearing 150 mph (running the engine above redline with the 3.54:1 rear end ratio). "A quiet muffler would be common courtesy and sensible public relations. Traffic driving is not much fun with the clutch location and high noise level, but the engine idles nicely at about 700 rpm and pulls well above 1,000 rpm... The SS is a truly tremendous machine at a very low price ($5,600), considering. On the other hand it is no dual-purpose car," the *R & T* staff concluded.

XK-SS production came to an abrupt halt on February 12, 1957: a fire swept through the factory and destroyed several parts of the production line and some 300 cars in various states of production, including several D-Types that were

ment in international motorsports, though it would continue to provide support to private entrants. Twenty-nine D-Types sat unsold (out of approximately sixty-seven "customer" units built), and Sir William was faced with a quandary: what to do with several dozen expensive, successful, yet not-in-demand race cars. Cannibalizing the already assembled cars made no sense, and a drastic discount price would only upset previous customers who had paid top dollar.

Only 7,500 Americans can get a new Jaguar this year . . .
You just can't mass produce a superb car like the new Jaguar XK150 Roadster.
Witness the painstaking workmanship, the clean, smooth-flowing lines, the sports
car simplicity. This newest Jaguar is the proud inheritor of Jaguar's racing tradi-
tions. Yet roominess, luxury and ease of handling make it the road car sans pareil.

In case you need an excuse to buy a Jaguar:

New features — New 4-wheel disc brakes, New one-piece wind screen, roll-up windows, convertible top. But the XK150 and XK150S retain all the Jaguar qualities connoisseurs cherish.

Performance — The famous Jaguar engine provides quiet surging power for starts and safe passing. The Jaguar suspension system prevents roll, pitching, wavering.

Resale Value — You get unbelievably high trade-in because Jaguar, the finest car of its class in the world, stands up for thousands of miles beyond expected "normal" standards.

The last of the original XK line, the XK 150. The 150 included features that would surface on the upcoming E-Type, such as four-wheel disk brakes and the 265 hp "S" version of the 3.8 XK engine. The flavor of this advertising art indicates Jaguar's attempt to appeal not only to "pure sports car" types, but also to those who enjoyed a little luxury with their sports.

being converted to XK-SSs. In total, it is said that sixteen XK-SSs were built, plus two D-Types that were converted to SS specs by the factory. It is likely that private owners converted cars back and forth between XK-SS and D-type trim as well, but suffice it to say that the XK-SS stands as Jaguar's rarest "production" model. Steve McQueen drove one, and in the opinion of the author, the SS remains one of the most desirable Jaguars ever.

E1A

Even for all its success, the D-Type's day was coming to an end. There were at least two major reasons, one involving engineering progress, and the other being timing, if nothing else.

The most limiting factor of the D-Type's design was its live rear axle. For long, smooth courses such as LeMans, it mattered little. On

shorter courses with tight turns and/or a lumpy surface, the D-Type garnered a reputation as being a bit jouncy, and with such substantial power on tap, getting the rear end of the car to "step around" was no trouble at all. Jaguar began testing an independent rear suspension as early as 1955.

The "timing" aspect of the equation was that, in response to the accident at the 1955 LeMans, prototype racers were now to be limited to 2.5 ltr, and there was suspicion that all other entrants would be limited to the same maximum displacement. While this did not happen—though displacement for production models was reduced to 3.0 ltr for 1958—the rumor spurred development of a new model incorporating an independent rear suspension and a 2.4-ltr version of the XK engine.

In late 1955, Phil Weaver, who managed the racing shop at Jaguar, sent a proposal to engineering chief Bill Heynes discussing a new model containing these features. Weaver further proposed that the model should be produced in both track and street versions. The shape once again was the responsibility of Malcom Sayer. Sayer not only "styled" cars, he calculated them. Preferring to be referred to as an "aerodynamicist," Sayer stretched and smoothed the D-Type's feline shape into the first "E1A" prototype ("E" being the "type," following the C and D-Types; "1" denoting the sequence of E-Type prototyping; and "A" reportedly referring to "aluminum," the material of which the car's skin was formed).

This car lacked many of the accouterments of a production vehicle, among them headlights. Viewed from the front, the arching fenders and small grille opening, sans headlights, gave the impression of an animal with no eyes; hence, the affectionate moniker "The Blind Mole."

E1A employed a center monocoque with deep sills, along with box-section front and rear bulkheads. Unlike the D-Type (and production E-Type), the forward tubular frame that carried the engine and front suspension was permanently fixed to the monocoque. The box-section part of the frame was assembled of magnesium tubing. As noted, a 2.4-ltr XK engine was employed, along with a standard four-speed transmission. The all-important independent rear suspension was part of the mix, though it did not yet include the rear subframe or the radius arms of the final

E-Type design. The car measured a scant 170 in long and was just over 5 ft wide—about 6 in shorter than a current Mercedes SL roadster, and only as wide as a Mazda Miata.

The car was tested extensively throughout 1957 and 1958, mostly at the hands of factory test driver Norman Dewis, though Heynes and even Sir William himself took turns at the wheel. Reports of those early tests were none too favorable: the car oversteered badly, rode harshly, the IRS was noisy, etc., though these are not atypical problems of development platforms. Soon-to-be World Driving champion Mike Hawthorn also tested the car. At least one and perhaps two other E1A type cars (which will be discussed in the next chapter) were constructed, but all in all, the E1A prototypes served as the evolutionary steps past the D-Type and the true development mules for the E-Type.

E2A

As the E1A prototype's development progressed, it became clearer that Jaguar had little intention of racing it. After Jaguar's withdrawal from racing in 1956 and the XK-SS project, the E1A continued its evolution into a street production that would replace the XK 120/140/150 line. It's somewhat curious, then, that during an acknowledged period of non-racing involvement, Jaguar would construct a one-off engineering prototype racer with a largely undeveloped engine, then entrust it to an American team to race at LeMans. Strange, but true.

E2A's layout included a monocoque center section, space frame front chassis, and all-alloy bodywork. A stabilizing fin even more pronounced than the D-Type's was mounted behind the driver, though the rear trunk line was interrupted by rather ungainly scoops, which provided cooling to the (inboard) rear brakes. Major differences between the E2A and the D-Type were the use of fully independent rear suspension—now quite similar to that which would appear on the production E-Type—and a 3.0-ltr version of the XK six featuring both aluminum block and head. Recall the post-1957 engine size limit of 3.0 ltr. Equipped with fuel injection and dry-sump lubrication, the engine produced horsepower reportedly in the 290 range—not much short of the previous 3.8-ltr D-Type's power output.

The car ran in the 1960 LeMans, entered by

JAGUAR

The XK engine also became the basis for a new line of small, sporty sedans which debuted in 1955. The original 2.4, and the 3.4 sedans, shown here, were immediate sales successes. With the introduction of the Mk 2 version in 1959, these earlier cars retroactively became referred to as Mk 1s, though the title was never officially applied.

the Briggs Cunningham operation, with Dan Gurney and Walt Hansgen driving. Though it showed early speed, running third early on, fuel injection problems caused a lean condition, burning pistons and the head gasket. One wonders what success might have been achieved if Jaguar had entered two or three cars, rather than just one somewhat untested machine.

Cunningham took E2A to the U.S. and retrofitted a D-type 3.8 engine, this to compete with machines regularly running in SCCA competition with up to 5.0-ltr engines. Hansgen was at the wheel as the car notched its only win, at Bridgehampton the same year. World driving champion Jack Brabham also competed with E2A at Riverside. By then, its day was done, as lighter, mid-engine machinery was soon to become the rage. Coventry sold E2A into a private collection.

The stage was set for the introduction of the E-Type in 1961.

The Lister Connection

It's one sort of challenge for a specialty or race car concern to design and build its own chassis. It also takes a certain ability for a cottage industry shop to pound out its own coachwork. But manufacturing one's own engine is an altogether more complex and expensive undertaking. Jaguar's racing successes in the 1950s were certainly made possible by the strong and sophisticated XK engine, and it's little wonder that small builders came knocking on William Lyons' door asking to purchase XK units for their own machines. In truth, more than a few probably obtained their XK engines at an even less glamorous venue: a local wrecking yard, from a car left for "breaking" as the British would say. This makes perfect sense, given the XK's ability to serve in Le Man-winning D-Types, or readily available sedans.

One such specialty builder was Brian Lister. Lister, of Cambridge, England, had done a bit of racing in the late 1940s, first in an MG-powered Cooper and later in a Tojeiro. He also employed other drivers, most notably Archie Scott-Brown, a gem of a pilot in spite of being born with only one hand. After convincing his father that the family engineering and production company should construct its own race cars as promotional items, Lister began building his machines in late 1953. The first Listers were powered by typical British powerplants of the time, either Bristol or MG units. These early efforts achieved moderate success in England throughout 1954 and 1955, the lighter Listers often beating the purebred Astons, Jaguar's own D-Types, and the occasional Maserati.

The first Jaguar-powered Lister was supposedly built by one of Lister's chassis customers. At the urging of British Petroleum (Lister's main supporter) Lister elected to purchase a 3.4 liter D-Type specification engine, thus paving the way for the "factory" Lister-Jaguars. The first such cars appeared in competition in early 1957. "Jaguar engines were the obvious choice for us," comments Brian Lister today, "because we knew they were reliable,

low in cost, and Jaguar would want to help as they had just retired from racing." Other choices were never seriously considered: "Astons were direct competitors and Chevrolet engines were not producing the power in '57, certainly not over here."

The cars were clever, if not particularly revolutionary. Built on a steel tube frame, with suspension via equal-length wishbones and coil springs up front, the car employed a de Dion with trailing arm setup in the rear. Twelve-inch Girling disc brakes were mounted all around, inboard at the rear. A production rack and pinion (usually Morris Minor) handled the steering chores, and a familiar knock-off 16-in Dunlop alloy wheel was found at each corner.

It's difficult to describe accurately the engine specifications, as the various cars came with different power plants depending on the customer's needs. Most were 3.4 D-Type units, running dry-sump oiling, triple side-draft 45 mm Weber carburetors, and a 10.0:1 compression ratio. This engine, as installed in a 1956 D-Type was rated at something just under 300 hp, although the Lister possessed a weight advantage over the factory Jaguar (1,900 lb versus approximately 2,200, depending upon trim and equipment). Backing the XK was a Jaguar racing four-speed box.

The measurements of the D-Type and Lister-Jaguar were similar, with the Lister just a 1/2 in longer (at 162 in) and 3 in narrower (62.5 in) although approximately 6 in lower (at just under 40 in). Road tests at the time put the Lister's 0–60 mph acceleration at 4.6 sec (*AutoSport*) and 0–100 mph at 10 sec flat (*Autocar*).

Although the D-type was Lister's natural benchmark, it's also interesting to compare the Lister-Jag with Lance Reventlow's Scarab. Indeed, the story goes that Reventlow visited Brian Lister with the intention of purchasing cars for competition in the U.S. He was said to be underwhelmed by the package and Lister's construction facilities. Lister doesn't particularly recall the visit: "our factory was old, built in 1890 and was very much an engineering works, with the usual swarf and car parts

Flavoring from the D-Type can be seen in the Lister–Jaguar's shape, though it's longer overall. Dunlop pin-drive knock-off wheels are almost identical. This particular 1958 Lister-Jag is owned by Eduardo Baptista of Mexico, and is driven here at the 1994 Monterey Historic Auto Races by that event's organizer, Steve Earle. *Author photo*

around. Not just a laboratory . . . which Reventlow was possibly looking for." To his credit, Reventlow built an exceptionally successful machine in its own right, though it was clearly inspired by what he saw at Lister.

Lister-Jaguars enjoyed considerable racing success in both the United States and Europe. In 1957, factory Listers notched European victories at Oulton Park, Goodwood, Crystal Palace, Snetterton, and others, winning eleven of thirteen races contested with Scott-Brown at the wheel! Needless to say, Lister became a rather in-demand constructor practically overnight.

The expected new-and-improved version appeared for 1958, designed by Lister himself and somewhat affectionately dubbed the "Knobbly" Lister, due to its bumpy (though many would say voluptuous) bodywork. High fender arches swelled over the front wheels, dropping low about the cowl, then swooping back up to cover the rear wheels before ending in a rounded, slightly upturned rump. It is this shape that most associate with the Lister-

Jaguar. The rear deck was about the same height as the windshield, and in combination with the reduced frontal aspect was Lister's attempt to improve the car's aerodynamic characteristics. The new coachwork could be had in either aluminum or magnesium. Wheelbase was increased 1-3/4 in and overall length by about 6 in. Engine's ranging form 3.0 to 3.8 ltr were available, and a turn-key Lister cost about $10,000.

Orders came pouring in from teams large and small, including the Le Mans winning Ecurie Ecosse and American Briggs Cunningham. Carroll Shelby, Jim Hall, and Cunningham also ordered cars with Chevrolet engines, but the Lister-Chevrolet is another story altogether (it never enjoyed the success of its Jaguar-engined sibling. The Cunningham/Lister Jags enjoyed particular success in America, with driver Walt Hansgen winning the SCCA Championship in 1958 and 1959. Various Lister-Jaguars competed at Le Mans the same two years, though none of the cars finished.

Nineteen fifty-nine turned out to be Lister's last: at Spa, Archie Scott-Brown had been dueling on and off with Masten Gregory, also in a Lister Jaguar. Rain plagued the event, and Scott-Brown lost control. After hitting a wall and flipping over an embankment, the car caught fire and Archie was badly burned. Gregory won the race; Scott-Brown died the following day. Ivor Bueb, who had driven a Lister-Jaguar at Le Mans, was killed in an F2 race the following Summer. Shortly thereafter, Lister left the automotive business. (Lister is no longer directly involved in the automobile business; his company produces food packaging equipment, and the Jaguar-powered Lister Storm is produced under license.)

What does the Lister-Jaguar story have to do with the E-Type? These machines served as a missing link between the all-conquering D-Types, and the Lightweight E-Types. The XK 150 certainly was not a racer, and the cars Brian Lister built served to keep Jaguar engine development moving ahead until the Lightweight Es came along.

JAGUAR 2

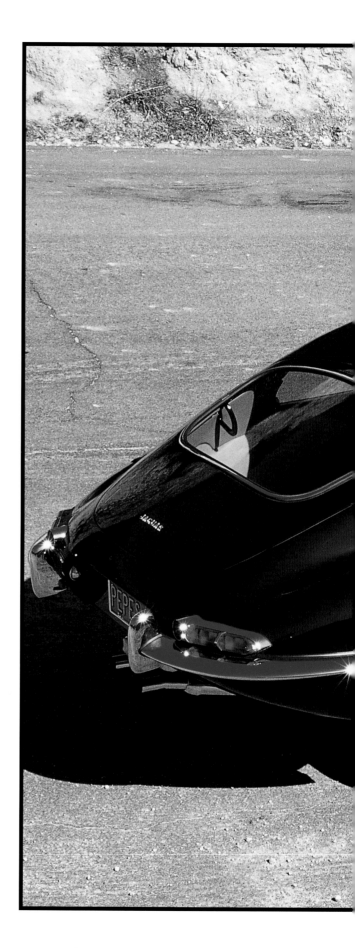

NEW JAGUAR XK-E COUPE. New 150-mile-per-hour Jaguar XK-E Coupe makes its world debut today. Car has 265 b.h.p. twin overhead camshaft engine, with three carburetors, straight port cylinder head and hemispherical combustion chambers; E-Type disc brakes all around and independent suspension systems on all four wheels. New body-chassis construction is stressed shell, all-steel monocoque design. Side-opening door in rear, incorporating window, gives access to luggage compartment. Interior has twin bucket seats, leather upholstery over foam rubber, tachometer, adjustable three-spoke steering wheel of polished alloy with wood rim, console for radio and twin speakers.
—U.S. Jaguar press release, from U.S. Headquarters, New York, March 15, 1961.

1961–1964 Series I 3.8

Given the amount of parentage outlined in the previous chapter, the E-Type required relatively little development time. After all, the engine and transmission would largely transfer over from the latest XK-150 S, and Jaguar had learned a great deal about chassis monocoque design and the independent rear suspension from the D-Type. This is not said to minimize in any way the effort and talent invested in the E-Type, but only to demonstrate that much of the car's design and hardware descended from its predecessors. It was not, nor did it need to be, a ground-up effort.

One interesting prototype was affectionately dubbed "The Pop Rivet Special." It was built essentially as a non-running mock-up in early 1958. Bill Heynes later chose to perform running

1963 Series I 3.8 Fixed-Head Coupe. *David W. Newhardt photo*

tests with the vehicle, so it was fitted with a drivetrain and the panels were pop riveted together; hence, the name.

According to Philip Porter, the first prototypes commonly thought of as production spec E-Types were chassis numbers 850001 and 850002, or "the blue car" and "the red car," respectively. Both were roadsters, the first fixed-head coupe being chassis number 885001, which is the gray car often seen in many early renderings. FHC chassis numbers 885002, 885003, and 885004 were variously used for testing and development and then were dolled up for the E-Type's premier at various international car shows. It's unlikely that some of today's hand-built, preproduction test machines would also serve show duty!

The E-Type brought together the best elements from its ancestors, cloaked in the now legendary coachwork designed by Malcom Sayer and, of course, inspired by Sir William Lyons. Though the roadster came first, it is the fixed-head coupe that was said to be Lyons' favorite of the two. The shape, expressing both feline and masculine character, was not only styled but calculated mathematically by Sayer for aerodynamic efficiency. Certainly inspired by the D-Type but smoother overall, the E-Type, at 175.3 in, measured a foot longer than its racing ancestor.

Unlike the D-Type, however, the E-Type's coachwork was rendered in all steel. Browns Lane did not have the capacity to stamp out all of the body panels, so outside vendors The Pressed Steel Company and Abbey Panels were subcontracted for most of the coachwork and pressings for the monocoque. The monocoque, comprising about two-thirds of the chassis, featured hollow

The E-Type's American debut at the New York Auto Show, 1961. The gown and the E-Type coupe were a matching bronze/gold color. The model for this particular launch was actress Marilyn Harold. *(Jaguar Cars Archives)*

sill sections (famous for their ability to trap water, then rust!), the floor, firewall, trunk area, and rear fenders. Most were stressed members, giving the E-Type considerable chassis rigidity for the era. Remember, this was before the days of computer aided design. It is said that little formal testing of the structure was done—except after the E-Type was in production.

To this "middle" and "rear" section of the car was attached a tubular front subframe, similar again to that of the D-Type though employing slightly thinner-gauge metal. This front frame section attached to the monocoque via bolting at eight pick-up points. This is why the E-Type is often referred to as a semi-monocoque design, as the front is comprised of the tube subframe, and the entire hood, hinged at the front, is an unstressed member. The hood is an interesting piece of coachwork in and of itself, made in three pieces and carrying no grillework of any kind. As the nose, engine cover, and front fenders all opened forward, access to the engine compartment and front suspension area was virtually unrestricted. The oval, open air intake, slim

Jaguar ad introducing the E-Type. Note that some advertising, even this early, began making reference to the car as an "XK-E."

chrome bumpers, and simply beautiful glass-covered headlights gave this earliest of E-Types a face to remember.

From an engineering standpoint, the combination monocoque-and-subframe design provided less torsional rigidity and stiffness than it would had Jaguar chosen to go with either a complete monocoque design or a full tube frame chassis. Pressed Steel did some test work in 1963 on bare E-Type chassis and concluded that the bolt-on arrangement was a bit of a structural liability.

From a production standpoint, this design would likely be a plus, as it would allow retooling the E-Type for different engines (which of course would happen some ten years later) without major changes to the monocoque portion of the chassis. On racing E-Types, it is common to weld and reinforce the connection at the attachment points. Still, it was an advanced design for the day, as full monocoque cars would not really become prominent until the mid-1960s, and Ferrari had some of its greatest success with pure tube frame cars. Few will argue, however, that

Malcolm Sayer, the self-described aerodynamicist who was also a major force in the styling of all Jaguar models, including the E-Type. Unlike most stylists who drew on paper or easels, Sayer, it is said, would often draw in full scale, on long rolls of paper or just on a long wall. He would also calculate the aerodynamic effects of various shapes mathematically—decades before the advent of computer-aided design (CAD) capability. *Jaguar Daimler Heritage Trust*

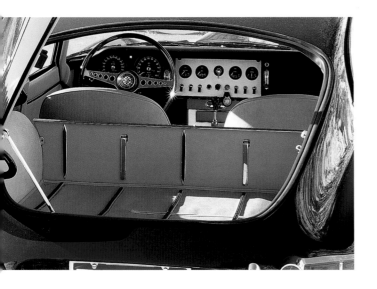

Coupe body style offers considerably greater luggage capacity than roadster; hatch door is unusual in that it is hinged at the side, rather than at the top, though it would be difficult to think of an E-Type as a "hatchback" under any circumstances. *David W. Newhardt photo*

when fully cloaked in either roadster or coupe bodywork, the E-Type stands as one of the most outstanding automotive designs of all time, having made more than its fair share of art museum appearances. It's certainly one of the few designs that, to most eyes, is as attractive in closed form as it is in open configuration. Though it was not quite the aerodynamic equal of its racing predecessor, its small frontal area and slippery shape still aided its performance and ultimate top speed

The 3.8 liter XK, as installed in Series I E-Types, is to some the best version ever. More than a few E-Type owners met their matches attempting to adjust and synchronize triple sidedraft SU carbs. Once set up properly (usually by an expert mechanic or the sharpest of do-it-yourselfers), the linkage tends to hold its tune very well. *Author photo*

Series I wire wheel with "ribbed" hub surface and eared knock-off nut; both would change on later models. Note original tread pattern Dunlop tires and Lucas lead-top battery on Ron Cressey's show-winning '63 roadster. *Author photo*

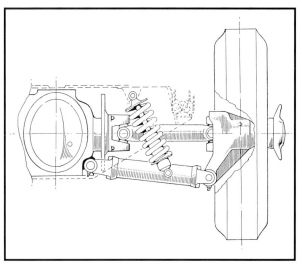

Cross section of rear suspension shows wheel centerline in relation to the hub carrier, half-shaft detail, and inboard disk brake. Dotted lines detail metal housing to which suspension mounts. Only one shock absorber is shown in this illustration, as the other would be directly behind it. *Jaguar Cars*

ability—important for bragging rights and a major selling feature in the early 1960s.

Front suspension architecture was virtually identical to the D-Type's, featuring double wishbone members and torsion bar springing. An antiroll bar was also included, as well as telescopic shock absorbers. Brakes are front disc, again in an era when many high-performance models still used drum brakes. The American firm Kelsey-Hayes, a leader in aircraft and racing brake application at the time, supplied the vacuum booster system providing power assist pressure to the dual master cylinders. The balance of the brake componentry was largely provided by Dunlop. Steering was via a manual rack and pinion design in order to provide sharp steering response and proper road feel.

The rear suspension was the much-heralded fully independent design, mounted in a stamped steel, detachable subframe, or "cradle." Essentially the design of R. J. "Bob" Knight, one of Jaguar's finer engineers, this type of suspension was a first for the company on a series production machine and quite revolutionary overall (most Ferraris of the day employed live axles). The central differential was of Salisbury "hypoid" design and featured a Power-lock limited slip. Damping was provided by coil over shock absorbers, two per side. Light cast-alloy hub car-

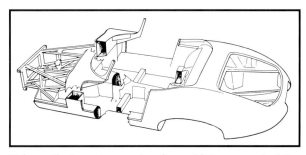

This particular cutaway drawing, which was part of the original launch press kit, details the monocoque's large, hollow bulkhead sections and sills. Unfortunately, all these areas can take on water in a big way and are the first areas that should be checked for rust when considering the purchase of an E-Type. The rocker panel sections are reasonably easy to replace, but other box sections in the floor and bulkhead area qualify as major restoration work and are quite expensive to put right. *Jaguar Cars*

riers reduced unsprung weight over a steel upright; the layout also employed a set of trailing arms and a rear antiroll bar. The disc brakes were mounted inboard in a further effort to reduce unsprung weight that would increase suspension response and result in improved handling.

The goal of such a sophisticated rear suspension package was of course to achieve the best possible balance between overall handling and ride comfort. So successful was this design that it was ultimately expanded to virtually the entire Jaguar line-up, first seen in the Mark X large sedan, also introduced in 1961. Soon, vari-

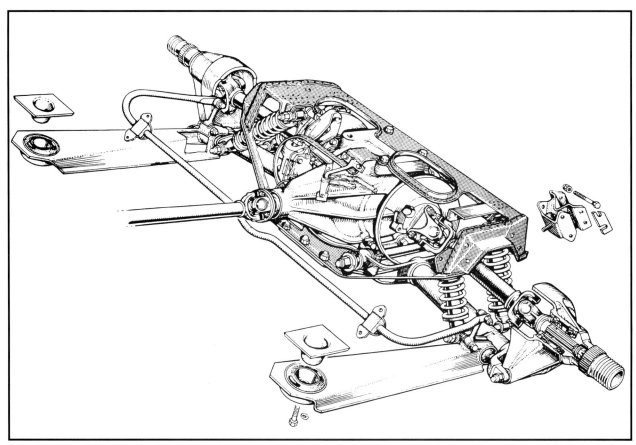

Steel subframe, or "cage," holds componentry of E-Type (and Mk X) independent rear suspension (IRS) unit: Salisbury differential, Dunlop inboard disk brakes, alloy hub carriers, radius arms, lower wishbone units, and anti-sway bar. Inboard brakes were not as affected by heat as one would expect, though servicing them properly required all but removal of the entire rear end assembly. A derivative of this design lives on in today's XJS, some thirty-five years after its introduction on the 1961 E-Type. *Jaguar Cars*

ations of the Mk 2 sedans (which employed half-leaf spring setups), dubbed the "3.4 and 3.8 S-Types," also made use of this E-Type-derived independent suspension; in 1968, the all-new XJ6 employed the same hardware. A very similar descendant of this original design is still in production, as of this writing, on the XJS—nearly thirty-five years after its debut on the E-Type!

For power, the E-Type of course employed the already legendary XK six-cylinder powerplant, in 3.8-ltr (actually 3781 cc) form. The engine had been continuously upgraded, for it had been in series production for more than ten years. As installed in the new E-Type, its configuration was virtually identical to that of its final appearance in the highest spec XK 150. Fed by three 2-in sidedraft SU carburetors, the engine carried a rating of 265 gross hp at 5500 rpm, with torque measuring 260 lb-ft at 4,000 rpm. Experts agreed, then as now, that this rating was at least a bit optimistic:

estimates of 230–250 hp are more realistic. Even at that, the power output was exceptional, especially given the E-Type's 1961 target cost of $5,595 (U.S.). Though the chart below is somewhat simplistic in representing only cubic inches, horsepower, and cost, it makes it clear that the E-Type offered performance potential equal or beyond that of many of its costlier rivals.

Model	Cubic Inches	Horsepower @ RPM	Cost
E-Type	231	265 @ 5,500	$6,000
Jensen 541S	244	150 @ 4,100	$7,750
Gordon-Keeble	283	230 @ 4,800	$8,526
Aston Martin DB4	224	263 @ 5,700	$10,400
Mercedes 300 SL	183	240 @ 6,100	$10,950

Again, perhaps a simple analysis, but certain evidence of the E-Type's value/performance potential.

Sports Cars Illustrated became *CAR and DRIVER* in May 1961, and put the "sensational Jaguar XKE!" on its cover. The very early model tested and photographed for this issue did not yet have the chrome bezels around the headlight covers.

The engine retained its basic architecture of an iron block, seven main-bearing crankshaft, an alloy double overhead cam head with hemispherical combustion chambers, etc. The standard compression ratio was 9.00:1, though 8.00:1 was an option (presumably for markets with lesser-quality fuel). The engine was cooled via a thermostatically controlled electric fan.

We'd be remiss in outlining the engine's specifications without putting in a word about its appearance. As much as the E-Type's shape

It's little wonder that the Jaguar IRS unit is exceptionally popular among hot rodders and kit car builders alike. Besides offering still-contemporary hardware, such as coil over shocks and inboard disk brakes, the unit is fairly easy to mate to just about anything because it is mounted on its own subframe. These assemblies have ended up under sports cars, Ford F-100 pick ups, replica Cobras, and any number of T-bucket-style hot rods.
David W. Newhardt photo

Jaguar elegance: The beauty that's more than skin-deep

Inspect each sweep, each curve, each fluid line of any Jaguar, and you bear witness to Jaguar elegance—a grace of styling that has been engineered from within the heart of the automobile itself. Jaguar elegance is reflected here in two exciting motor cars. One, the new Jaguar XK-E, is available either as an open sports roadster with interchangeable soft or hard top or a completely enclosed *Gran Turismo* coupe. For the family man who requires a roomier vehicle, there is the versatile Jaguar 3.8 Sedan. Pure Jaguar from the word go, this car has been titled "the sedan that behaves like a sports car." Discover Jaguar elegance yourself. See and drive either of these fine Jaguars soon at your local dealer's. JAGUAR CARS INC., 32 East 57th Street, New York 22, N.Y.

Technical Service and Parts Headquarters, 42-50 Twenty-First St., Long Island City 1, N.Y.

Jaguar was awash in either new or recent, and very successful, models in the early 1960s. The former 2.4 sedan became the Mk 2 in 1959 and was ultimately offered with the 3.8-ltr engine. The graceful but aging body-on-frame Mk IX was replaced by the unit-bodied, full-independent suspension Mk X, and of course the E-Type replaced the last of the XK line-up. All three would continue to be the mainstays of Jaguar's model roster through introduction of the XJ6 in 1968.

Chevrolet made quite a bit of noise about its 283 hp, 283 ci, fuel-injected V-8 engine putting out one horsepower per cubic inch in 1957. A justifiable boast for sure, but the 3.8 E-Type's rating of 265 hp and 230 ci gave it bragging rights to about 1.15 horsepower per cubic inch—that is, if the 265 bhp rating was to be believed. Many contemporary experts place the actual output of factory engines at about 240 gross horsepower. *Jaguar Archives*

exuded beauty from nearly any angle, its engine bay was one that any sports car buyer would be proud of. The symmetry of the cam covers was set off by their polished finish, and the intricacy of the carburetor linkage displayed a certainly mechanical beauty as well. At a time when dual carburetors were still a flight of fancy to many American buyers, the E-Type had *three*—their exotic appearance further enhanced by a hood that tilted forward to reveal the entire engine. Besides a shape that looked fast, the E-Type had an *engine* that looked fast.

Backing the engine was a Moss four-speed manual transmission—the only choice, as no automatic transmission was offered (at the time) and overdrive was really not required. Power transferred through a 10 in Borg & Beck dry plate clutch. The Moss box's biggest deficiencies were that it employed no first gear synchromesh and that it also put out considerable gear whine in the same ratio. Still, it had proven itself well in competition, being exceptionally durable and reliable, and having gear ratios well suited to the 3.8's power characteristics. The standard ratio for the

Behind the Wheel:
1964 E-Type 3.8 Roadster

Many enthusiasts refer to the early Series I as the "Elemental E-Type," an accurate description in so many ways. Being the first iteration of the design, it could be philosophically considered the most uninhibited interpretation of the maker's vision. The metal console is a sharp contrast to the later, softer-looking upholstered units. There was none of the safety or special emissions gear to be found on later cars. Those simple chrome bumpers. No power steering.

Debate will always rage as to whether the 3.8 or the 4.2 engine is better, but it's commonly acknowledged that the 3.8 gives up some low end torque for some top end power and revs. Even more commonly agreed upon is that the later Jaguar all-synchro four-speed is clearly easier to live with than the Moss-sourced box found in the early cars.

The dash-mounted starter button, a touch somewhat missed on the Series III machines, sort of "ca-chonks" the 3.8 to life; the exhaust note is deep, yet noticeably sharper than that of the later six-cylinder cars. Depressing the clutch presents no drama, though the Moss is a bit tougher to coax into first. The instant the car rolls, you hear it: that much heralded first gear whine. Its pitch rises higher with speed, sounding much like a supercharger engaged for only first gear. Negotiating gears two through four is much less work.

The engine in this particular machine idles easily and pulls strongly to past 5000 rpm. For all the talk about how wonderful BMW straight sixes are (and they are), the XK's song is also magic, especially top down, with a soft burble on overrun. It feels quick, and fast by the standards of any era, certainly by those of the early '60s.

The cockpit is snug, or intimate, depending upon your size and attitude about such things. These Series I seats, smallish in the hips and low at the squab, were deemed uncomfortable by some early road testers, though they felt fine to this backside. Visibility is excellent—what else, it's a roadster! Readability of the main gauges through the handsome alloy and wood steering wheel is fine, something not so easily said for many "exotics" of the era.

While the handling certainly feels dated today, it was heralded as nothing short of spectacular thirty years ago. The narrow wire wheels and 185-section tires set the cornering limits, and there's more body roll than I would care for, but the suspension does a remarkable job of keeping all four wheels planted during spirited driving. The IRS also maintains constant camber, though front-to-rear weight transfer under hard acceleration is not well controlled.

Steering gets little better than this, at just about any price: direct, light at low speeds, yet maintaining firm touch at higher speeds. Braking feels strong and sure, though it takes a bit of pedal before the binders take hold—perhaps just an anomaly of this particular car. With the top down, you can just about forget conversation at anything more than 65 mph, but who cares?

All in all, a nostalgic, sporty, quasi-luxurious, and sometimes thrilling machine to drive. What could be better? The same car with a later transmission installed!

---

final drive was. 3.31:1, though a half-dozen higher and lower ratios were offered as options, depending upon the owner's intended use (racing?) and the country in which the car was sold. The finishing touch? The chromed, genuine knock-off Dunlop 15-in wire wheels, of course.

Interior accommodations were an artful blend of luxury, sport, and function. As always, Jaguar employed a full range of gauges, placing the Smiths tachometer and speedometer directly in front of the driver, in perfect view within the now-classic polished alloy/mahogany steering

Factory press photo of RHD roadster interior and facia detail. This particular car was registered "1600RW" and was an early press test car. Symmetry of dashboard and instrument placement made for easy production of both right- and left-hand-drive versions. *(Jaguar Cars Archives)*

wheel. The wheel, drilled more for appearance than genuine weight savings, mounted on a telescoping column. Ancillary gauges for charging, oil pressure, temperature, and fuel tank were carried in a center-mounted console fascia also containing the headlight switch, ignition key, and starter button. Below the gauges was a symmetrically placed row of toggle switches for interior lights, heater fan, etc. Even the choke and heater controls were placed symmetrically on either side of the fascia.

Several other interior controls reinforced the E-Type's position as both a serious performance machine and one with luxury aspirations. Map and interior lights were included, as was an electric clock. A "flash function" was incorporated into one of the stalks, and a warning light indicated low brake fluid levels. Speakers were built into the console; the radio installation was left to the dealer or owner. A cigar lighter and windshield washer were standard; such items were not available, or were offered only at extra cost, on many more expensive machines. Over-

all, a classic dash layout if there ever was one.

Genuine wood trim, a common and popular feature in Jaguars then as now, was conspicuous by its absence in the E-Type. The aforementioned center console and fascia were covered by "pebble finish" aluminum panels. Leather, another Jaguar hallmark, was employed for covering the seating surfaces, portions of the console, and other interior trim. High-quality vinyls covered door panels and the balance of the interior; several interior colors could be selected with color-keyed cut pile carpeting, though the dashboard areas were always trimmed in black.

It is now common to see an automobile introduced first in coupe version, with the convertible to follow a year or two on; the most

Next page, the Series I coupe was said to be William Lyons' favorite E-Type, but the shape translated masterfully to open form. The rear fenders flow into the daintiest of shapes; unfortunately, the slenderness of the rear bodywork makes for a trunk best suited for briefcases. Still, a landmark shape then and now. *Author photo*

Race-inspired aluminum finish on center dash area and console is handsome, but casts considerable reflection at the driver's eyes—especially in an open car at sunset. Metal dash would be replaced on later 4.2 cars. Radios were dealer-installed, though twin console-mounted speakers were standard equipment. Note virtually perfect symmetry of the overall dash design: exactly two gauges and three rocker switches on each side of the light switch, etc. Even the heater controls and choke lever look as similar as possible. *Author photo*

Concours presentation of original tool roll, jack, and warranty book. The warranty book also contained a set of coupons reminding the owner of scheduled service items and their mileage intervals. Knock-off hub mallet is rolled rawhide on one side, bronze on the other. *Author photo*

recent iterations of the Chevrolet Camaro and BMW 325i are but two examples. But Jaguar chose to bring out the full line: both the coupe, with its side-hinged rear hatch, and the roadster, featuring a folding canvas top and an optional, removable, fiberglass hardtop.

The E-Type premiered at major auto shows and salons around the world, though its two most significant intros were certainly in Geneva, Switzerland, and at the U.S. debut in New York. The Geneva Auto Show was held in the middle of March 1961, and though many motoring journalists had knowledge of the E-Type's development (Christopher Jennings of *The Motor* had been loaned the E1A prototype in 1958—and had kept the fact quiet for nearly three years!), the public was largely unaware of what "the new Jaguar sports car" would be. In short, the press, commentary, and public reaction to the gun-metal gray prototype coupe would fill a book. Simply put, the world's wire services were lit with glowing, adjective-laden euphoria over the new E-Type.

England's weekly automotive journal, *The Motor*, was as enthusiastic as any:

Announcing the most advanced sports car in the world. No more famous background can be found anywhere than that which lies behind the Jaguar "E" Type G.T. (Grand Touring) models. Developed from the famous "C" Type and "D" Type Sports Racing Cars with their illustrious records of successes on the race tracks of the world, the "E" Type G.T. Models are presented as elegant and luxuriously appointed road vehicles having an outstanding road performance and incorporating very many features derived from the vast store of experience gained in international competitive events . . . A study of the complete description and technical data contained in this issue of the 'Motor' will reveal that, in every particular, from basic principles to minute details, the Jaguar "E" Type G.T. is, in truth, the most advanced sports car in the world.

William "Bill" Heynes was perhaps the most instrumental force in Jaguar's post-WW II development direction and success: an engineer and designer who knew the considerable value that competition wins and performance development could add to the marque's image. Heynes and "Lofty" England ensured that Sir William Lyons' visions, Malcolm Sayer's shapes, and the efforts of the rest of the Jaguar development and engineering staffs actually became production automobiles. *Jaguar Daimler Heritage Trust*

While Jaguar's marketers would have been foolish not to capitalize on the E-Type's appearance, advertising copy also included a somewhat technical discussion of its engineering features. In this particular ad, the benefits of the independent rear suspension are extolled.

Another interesting advertising effort playing upon Jaguar's feline namesake and character, this 1964 ad ranks as one of the best ever for the E-Type. It was honored by inclusion in an exhibit of American advertising at the Louvre in Paris. The overall shape is obscured, though there's certainly no difficulty in determining the model. A few interesting pricing notes: the coupe was still an exceptionally reasonable $5,625—with the roadster priced at $200 *less*.

The *Daily Express*, an English newspaper, proclaimed in a headline that the "new Jaguar Can Beat the World at 140 mph and not a Rival anywhere." The article informed its readers that "Bill Lyons, head of Jaguars, staggered Europe's leading car experts at the preview of the Geneva Motor Show Today. He exhibited a brand new car with a performance that equals, or is better than, any out-and-out sports car in the world. Yet this one is a ground touring car . . . The new Jag will leap from zero to 100 miles an hour, through the gears, in less than a quarter of a minute—14.6 seconds."

The *Daily Mirror* concluded, "Here is a new British Sports car, so fast that when it takes the road most drivers will get only a REAR view . . . it is capable of 150 miles an hour, say the makers. The Jaguar E will be put on the American market soon. It will be the fastest mass-produced sports car ever offered for sale in America." Author Philip Porter went on to quote Bill

Heynes' reaction to questions about the importance of the American market to Jaguar and the E-Type: "At this stage, it is really impossible to tell how the American market will react. We are very hopeful, of course, but the U.S. holds the key to the situation."

As mentioned, the E-Type was essentially introduced to the American market at the New York International Automobile Show, just a month (April 1961) after the car's introduction in Europe. Jaguar sent no less than four prototype and early production E-Types to New York, and the result was no less astonishing than it was in Geneva. Crowds fought for glimpses of this newest Jaguar, and as soon as the cars were available for road testers, the accolades poured forth from the American enthusiast press.

Car and Driver, which had just changed

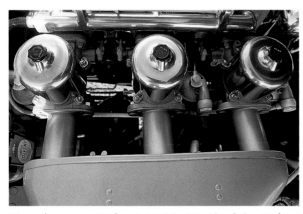

Three in a row: An important hallmark of the Series I XK engine is the triple sidedraft SU carbs. What appear to be small bolt heads at the tops of the carbs are actually plungers that must be unscrewed, opening a port by which the oil for the dampers is checked and filled. *David W. Newhardt photo*

The central area of the dash facia is business-only and obviously race-inspired; it puts the two most important gauges directly in front of the driver. Both are easily visible through the steering wheel, and the clock occupies a handy location at the bottom of the tachometer. *David W. Newhardt photo*

its name from *Sports Car Illustrated*, put the E-Type on its cover, and noted racing journalist/photographer Jesse Alexander started right off by saying "This is the most exciting sports car news of 1961 . . . Rumors about the XKE have been flying for months. When Briggs Cunningham entered one of the prototypes (E2A) at Le Mans last year, tongues wagged even harder, and it was thought that its introduction was imminent." Alexander summarized *C&D's* first take on the E-Type: "The specs are sensational; that such a car could be engineered is remarkable. As usual, Jaguar adds a minor miracle by selling such a machine at an incredible price. The XKE is not expected to cost appreciably more than the XK 150S, top car of the series it completely replaces! This means we're talking about $5,500 . . . dramatic tribute to the policies of Jaguar's Sir William Lyons."

Road & Track was no less impressed. "Sensational is the word for this Coventry cat. If a new car ever created greater excitement around our office than the new Jaguar XK-E, we can't remember it. And to sum up this car in the third sentence of a report may be unusual for us, but it is easy to do. The car comes up to, and exceeds, all our great expectations." *R&T* noted that "in driving the car for the first time, the superb riding qualities do indeed make an immediate impression. In fact, the ride is so good we will say without equivocation that only one other sports car has a comparable ride, and it also has inde-

pendent suspension on all four wheels . . . what is even more remarkable is the car's uncanny adhesive characteristics."

R&T went on to add that "the steering also rates as very close to, if not actually, the best we have experienced. There is just the right amount of road feel, no kickback, moderate parking effort and a ratio that is quick without being too sensitive or tricky at high speed." The article concluded, simply, that "the Jaguar XK-E is one of the most exciting sports cars ever produced." High praise indeed.

A strike at the body production facility caused a bit of a delay in bringing E-Types to market, but by mid-1961 cars were beginning to flow into the pipeline. It was also early on that Jaguar took the opportunity to make several significant detail changes to the car before it went into full-scale series production.

Among the most visible changes was moving the exterior hood latches to the inside footwells, a look which was certainly neater, from a stylistic and security standpoint. No longer was the separate "T" handle tool required, as the new latch mechanism included an integrated handle. Another update was stamping the ventilation louvers directly into the hood; on approximately the first 500 cars, the louvers were stamped as separate pieces of metal, then welded in place. The earliest 1961 E-Types are often referred to as "flat floor" models, as by 1962 the pressings for the footwells were modified to drop the floor level

E-Type Lightweight: Jaguar's GTO?

Many processes in life are politically inspired, driven, and often manipulated. Corporate takeovers, world revolutions, election campaigns, etc. Race car homologation rules can easily be added to the list, though most takeovers, revolutions, and campaigns tend to be a bit less complicated! The administration of the homologation, technical inspection, and sanctioning of racing has driven constructor, drivers, fans, and officials equally crazy almost since the dawn of racing itself. One of the manufacturers most capable of navigating through, and occasionally around, the rule book was Ferrari, particularly in the hotly contested arena of international sports car racing in the 1960s.

Among the rules in place for the 1963 season was that in order to qualify a particular model for competition in the GT class, 100 "production" units had to be built. In all its different models, including post-1963 iterations, there were only forty Ferrari 250 GTOs built, but the model was cleared for competition. Go figure. Jaguar had been maintaining its non-involvement in racing since late 1956. This is not hard to imagine, as the company had won Le Mans five times in the previous decade, was riding the coattails of those success, and had invested considerable time, money, effort, and production capacity into bringing out both the E-Type and the all-new Mk X sedan at the beginning of the 1960s—not to mention a bit of remodeling at Browns Lane due to the 1957 fire. Racing? Who had time?

Lightweight chassis # S850663 with Sayer aerodynamic bodywork, among the most prized of the series. This car was driven in World Championship sports car races by Peter Sargent and Peter Lumsden. It is shown here competing at the Monterey Historic Auto Races. Unlike most Lightweights, which have fixed hardtops on roadster bodies, this is one of the cars to have scratch-built alloy coachwork. As of this writing, the car resides in Southern California. *Author photo*

With Mercedes essentially out of international competition, Ferrari was quickly becoming a very worthy adversary, and the now-legendary 250 GTO was an instant high watermark by late 1962. Though Jaguar was not at the time willing to re-enter racing with factory-supported teams and purpose-built models, it was willing to produce (or convert from street specification) a handful of "special build" competition cars for favored privateers, embracing some or all of the equipment that the factory had homologated for the 1963 season. The story goes that Jaguar employed some Ferrari-like methodology in getting through homologation by essentially submitting the lightweight specials as standard cars and the production E-Types as the specials. Rummaging through the archival records of the sanctioning bodies (if any exist) would likely yield some rather intriguing paperwork.

The cars were colloquially dubbed "Lightweight E-Types," though no such moniker was ever formally applied by the factory. The cars did exhibit special serial numbers, and they got their name from the extensive use of aluminum and various alloys in their construction. We'll say right now that it's likely no two of these cars were the same (more details to follow), but most of the Lightweights made use of alloy monocoque, bodywork, and engine block which combined to save approximately 500 lb over the weight of a standard E-Type. A few of the cars retained steel chassis and offered lesser weight-savings.

The Lightweight obviously sprang from the production model, but its inspiration lay in the D-Type, the E2A prototype, and a particularly successful E-Type campaigned by privateer John Coombs. Coombs ran drophead chassis # S85006, which carried the public relations-minded registration number of "BUY 1." Nineteen fifty-nine Le Mans Winner Roy Salvadori raced the car quite successfully throughout 1961, even though the production E-Type was not equipped as a pure racer. After the close of the season, Jaguar and Coombs performed substantial upgrades, including a monocoque of lighter-gauge steel as well as an aluminum hood and hardtop. Out went the standard 3.8's cylinder head, on went a D-Type head and

triple 45 DC03 Weber sidedraft carbs. Flared fenders covered alloy Dunlop knock-off wheels and racing tires were added later. Upgraded brakes, plastic windows, and a larger competition fuel tank essentially completed the transformation. Now re-registered as "4 WPD," this machine is commonly acknowledged as the first Lightweight E-Type. Through 1964, it was also driven by Graham Hill, Dan Gurney, and Jackie Stewart, among others.

Another of the most famous early Lightweights was Chassis EC1001, often referred to as the "Low Drag Coupe." Malcolm Sayer designed an aerodynamically more efficient roofline, more so than even that found on the fixed-head coupe. It is said that four cars of this configuration were to be built, though only one was completed and another (chassis S850063) was later modified to a similar specification. The latter was sold to and campaigned by Jaguar dealer Dick Protheroe, and in this author's opinion, it remains one of the most interesting E-Types ever built.

As noted, not all of the cars came in the same specification. Some had steel monocoques, some employed aluminum. Most employed an all-alloy engine featuring Lucas individual port fuel injection and a ZF five-speed transmission, though some ran iron blocks, Weber carbs, etc. The injected alloy block units produced between 330–350 hp.

Considering that the Lightweights enjoyed only half-baked support from Browns Lane, there were some significant victories and finishes. Three Lightweights were sold to (or at least run by) Briggs Cunningham, who competed with them at Le Mans, Sebring, and several other American venues. Curiously enough, two of the cars were campaigned by a total of four drivers all named Peter. S850663, referenced above, was driven by Peter Lumsden and Peter Sargent. It was nearly totaled at the Nurburgring in 1963, but was rebuilt at the factory and later updated to a fastback configuration similar to that of the Low Drag Coupe. Much of the aerodynamic work was developed by Dr. Samir Klat. Germans Peter Lindner and Peter Nocker competed in chassis S850662. It was factory-fitted with Low Drag roof structure

continued on next page

and competed at Le Mans in 1964. Lindner, driving the car at the Montlhery circuit in England, crashed heavily and lost his life in the incident. This machine was later rebuilt by Lynx engineering, which also makes splendid reproduction period Lightweights.

Interestingly, one Lightweight, chassis S850668, was essentially never run in competition, save for a hillclimb or two. It spent many years in museums around the world, and probably remains the most original Lightweight. *Classic and Sports Car* magazine staged a competition between this Lightweight, an Aston Martin Zagato, and a short-wheelbase Ferrari 250 GT for its June 1987 issue. Though a 250 GTO and a DB4/GT might have been a more appropriate for the comparison, the Ferrari and Aston were more than representative of the competition a Lightweight was likely to meet.

In short, the E-Type simply stormed the other two, running 0–60 mph in 5.0 sec, 0–100 mph in a mere 11.8 sec, and achieved a top speed of nearly 160 mph. The best estimate on Lightweight production is twelve cars plus the Low Drag Coupe, according to Phil Porter's *Jaguar E-Type: The Definitive History*. Other guesses range from ten to fourteen cars, though they may or may not include the Low Drag Coupe, the Coombs car, or others converted by the factory to Lightweight spec.

Fantastic as it was, the Lightweight never really had a shot at great success. It was, no matter how heavily modified, based upon a street-production car, rather than being a purpose-built racing machine. Mid-engined racers were quickly to become the rage, as would V-8 and V-12 engines. Jaguar certainly did not invest the effort (or money) it would have taken to make them world-beaters. And then there were those pesky GTOs that had a way of winning just about everything in sight, no matter who else showed up to race.

Lightweight E-Type Chassis # S850666, originally sold to Peter Sutcliffe. It was raced in Europe during 1963, then went to South Africa for various local competitions. It later returned to England and is said to now reside in the United States. Note modification to what appear to be nearly production-specification Series II open headlights, and small plastic spoiler on hood to help keep windshield clean during long endurance races. *Jaguar Daimler Heritage Trust*

by approximately two inches. This change increased legroom and seating position comfort. The pebble grain finish on the aluminum dash pieces gave way to more of a "diamond" pattern, and upholstery padding, piping, and sewing patterns were also changed. There were many other running detail changes early on, and indeed several hundred throughout the model's production history, but their bit-by-bit chronology is best left to the restoration guides.

Suffice it say that this newest Jaguar had arrived; and it was a hit.

The front-hinged bonnet certainly contributed to the purity of the E-Type's overall shape. It would have been difficult, if not impossible, to cleanly incorporate a hood opening, as the fenders and bonnet flow together as one. Doors open wide enough, but it still takes a careful step to get legs and feet across the wide sill area and into the recessed footwells. *Author photo*

JAGUAR 3

There ain't no substitute for cubic inches.
—popular hot-rodding axiom

1965–1967 Series I 4.2

Nothing is perfect, and the E-Type, for all its styling, performance, and value-for-cost, certainly wasn't. After approximately three years of production (considering that 1961 was really an introductory/development year, and the car got a late start), Jaguar management could see where the car could stand improvement. 1965 and 1966 would both be landmark model years for the E-Type, not only in terms of upgrading and improvement, but for expanding the car's market appeal—and increasing sales.

Nineteen sixty-five brought no new model per se; there were virtually no major styling changes, and the same coupe and roadster comprised the line-up. The major changes, and most of the minor ones, were mechanical, centering primarily around a larger version of the now-venerable XK powerplant, a new transmission, and some much needed upgrading in the electrical department. The interior also received significant changes.

No one would term the 3.8-ltr XK "down on power." Keep in mind that it was more and more often being pressed into service in larger, heavier sedans, often with automatic transmissions. Also

This particular Primrose Yellow, late-production 1967 model features the uncovered headlights yet is pure Series I in all other details. In this age of 5 mph bumpers, it would be hard to imagine a more harmonious frontal aspect than that of early E-Types. *Author photo*

From this angle, this late-1967 coupe is virtually indistinguishable from earlier models. The exhaust system employs "short" megaphones, as opposed to those on earlier cars where the "glasspack" section of the rear muffler was several inches longer. Chrome tubing between rear bumper overridders is an aftermarket piece. *Author photo*

The 4.2's seats had longer, lower cushions; adjustability for rake; and a new stitching pattern for their leather coverings. Wooden shift knob is an aftermarket piece. *Author photo*

at issue were the driving habits of the E-Type's largest market, the United States, comprised of a buyer group that was used to the copious torque available at low RPMs from American V-8s. A larger bore for the 3.8 created more cubic inches and more torque at lower revs, plain and simple.

The re-engineering effort invested in the engine was more than just a 5 mm bore increase (from 87.00 to 92.07 mm), though the already longish stroke remained unchanged. Using a completely new engine block was out of the question, so the cylinder bores were somewhat "siamesed" together to allow for the larger bore. This necessitated a new crankshaft; pistons and rings were redesigned to reduce oil consumption, another feature of the

3.8 that American buyers were not used to.

They were most likely budgetary restrictions that precluded a new head design. Given the revised bore centers on four of the cylinders, the combustion chambers for those same cylinders did not quite line-up, being about 3/16 in off—not exactly elegant design, but apparently compression was unaffected. Additional modifi-

cations to the block allowed for better water circulation in the interest of improved cooling, another problem afflicting the earliest E-Types. The new engine, dubbed the "4.2," was actually 4235 cc, or 258 ci.

As noted, the goal was not so much an increase in power output (in fact, the maximum rating of 265 gross hp did not change, though it

Wheels on this late-1967 car are a cross between those of the Series I and Series II cars that would follow. The two-pronged knock-offs are the same as the earlier cars', though the "flat surface" of the inner hub area is straight from the 1968 and later cars. *Author photo*

Advertisement for the-new-for-1965 2+2 makes its market intentions clear with its first word: "Detroit." The slogan "A different breed of cat," from previous ads, had also caught on, and was carried over to many later promotional materials.

was now peaking at 5,400, instead of 5,500) so much as the change in the torque level and where it was felt in the powerband. The 4.2 was rated at 283 lb-ft, vs. the 3.8's 261 lb-ft rating at the same 4,000 rpm, an increase of about ten percent.

While some Jaguar engineers reportedly questioned the need for the larger engine's installation in the E-Type, nobody complained about an all-new, Jaguar-designed and -built four-speed transmission replacing the former Moss box. The Moss unit was race-proven and tough, but it lacked synchromesh in first gear. Equally annoying was the considerable gear whine created while in that same low ratio. More than a few E-Type clutches were blown because of a driver being unable to engage first (or unwilling to put up with the noise) and just revving the engine while slipping the hapless clutch for a less-than-smooth getaway. A 10-in Laycock diaphragm clutch made for lower pedal pressures and a slightly quicker takeup.

The electrical upgrades were also significant. The 3.8 E-Types had all been positive ground (or "positive earth," as the British said) but the new 4.2 cars were all negative ground. The change aided in the troubleshooting of electrical gremlins, something for which British cars, Jaguars included, have become rather famous. A more powerful Lucas alternator was fitted, which provided a higher power output at lower rpm than the previous generator. A supposedly more

reliable SU fuel pump arrangement replaced the prior tank-immersed Lucas unit.

Other related mechanical changes included swapping the Kelsey-Hayes bellows-type brake booster for a Lucas vacuum booster, designed for greater line pressure with less pedal effort. The brake discs, calipers, and other related hardware remained largely unchanged.

The most noticeable change to the cabin was the doing away with the patterned aluminum coverings on the center of the dash and parts of the console (actually, the last of the 3.8 cars had received this treatment as well). These items were now covered in a pebble-grained black vinyl. The prior seat design was criticized as being uncomfortable and a bit short on support, so an all-new seat, with adjustable back and revised leather pattern, was included in the new interior. An upholstered armrest/storage binnacle appeared on the console between the seats. Small covers were added to the hinges for the

Jaguar factory photo of new 4.2 XK engine. Factory press material noted that it was "designed to give the car greater acceleration, particularly in the lower and mid- speed ranges. Coupled to the engine is a buttery smooth, all synchromesh four-speed gearbox." Note alternator replacing previous generator. *Jaguar Archive*

rear hatch, and for the first time, air conditioning was an available option for left-hand drive cars.

So, was the new 4.2 better than the 3.8? Yes. And no.

In most instances of "everyday" driving— even in a spirited manner—the 4.2 held a slim but measurable advantage over its smaller-engined predecessor, at least based on the following table:

	1964 3.8	1966 4.2
0–30 mph	2.9 sec	2.5 sec
0–60 mph	7.4 sec	7.1 sec
0–100 mph	19.0 sec	19.6 sec

Source *Road & Track, Car and Driver*

The 4.2 certainly delivered its power at RPM levels and in a manner more in keeping with the way American customers drove. Journalist Pete Lyons, in a retrospective on the E-Type for *Car and Driver*, contrasted the two engines beautifully: "It (the 3.8) was built with a completely different tuning philosophy. The later 4.2 is a punchy, low end torquer; revs over 4,000 feel superfluous. The 3.8 has plenty of low-end too, but it brightens distinctly at 3,500 rpm and pulls toward its 5,500 redline with energetic enthusiasm." Continued Lyons, "Where the 4.2 feels and often sounds like a gas turbine, the 3.8 is unmistakably still a piston power plant—and one that preserves the rorty, rasty nature of its racing heritage."

Behind the Wheel:
1967 E-Type 2+2 Automatic

Some E-Type purists dismiss the automatic transmission, six-cylinder 2+2 as a "lounge lizard." "They're heavier than a coupe or roadster, and well, *real* sports cars *don't* have slushboxes," they say. Or other favorites: "It's an old man's sports car"; "It's not as pure of line as the original."

While these and other callous complaints are certainly a matter of personal opinion, this author feels that *any* E-Type is indeed a sports car, for a man or woman of any age, and the lines look just fine, thank you. True, the few extra pounds take a little edge off acceleration, and rowing through a post-1965 E-Type's manual box is an undeniable pleasure. Still, for some enthusiasts, the automatic box, long-wheelbase E-Type still has a lot to offer.

The first impression comes from inside: no longer is any driver cramped for leg room, and the taller pilot will notice significantly more headroom than is found in a Series I coupe. The view from the driver's seat is the same, and you're hard-pressed to notice that the rear window is now a bit farther back. A larger brake pedal replaces that of the stick shift model. The shifter for the BW automatic falls neatly to hand. The shift pattern is similar to that of a Ford C-4 automatic of the same era: "D1" gives a 1-2-3 gear progression, whereas "D2" starts off in second then shifts to third. Select Low from a stop, and that's all you get. But shift into "L" at speed, and you get second gear—only down to about 25 mph, when the box drops back in to low again. Confusing? More than it should be, and it never allows straight 1-2-3 manual gear selection like some of today's best sporting automatics.

The above complaining aside, gear ratios seem ideally matched to the XK's low end torque. Shifts are crisp at light throttle, though if you accelerate hard and then let off just prior to a shift, the next gear comes with a bang. Passing is no problem, as flooring the throttle brings a 3-2 downshift and plenty of rpm. An overdrive gear would be welcome for really relaxed cruising, but four-speed overdrive automatics were a few years off yet.

Handling at the limit is most likely sacrificed incrementally at the expense of a smoother ride. The longer wheelbase seems to smooth out the freeway hop sometimes noticed in an early 3.8 car, and the extra room is usually welcomed by American-sized drivers. Turn-in is not as crisp, however, the longer wheelbase perhaps accentuating the E-Type's narrow track.

The car's extra seating area is a "+2" at best, well suited for children under ten or petite, limber adults with senses of humor. Still, with the seat squab moved into the forward position, luggage space is increased dramatically over a coupe's.

The 2+2 is certainly not the most stimulating E-Type, but it is perhaps the most pleasant, and it's still an E-Type, which makes it more satisfying to drive than many a machine. It's a cruiser, not a racer, but what's wrong with that?

While Jaguar enthusiasts will debate the relative merits of the 3.8 versus the 4.2 seemingly forever (there is also a cadre of folks who maintain that the 3.4 is actually the best overall version of the XK, though certainly not the most powerful), few will argue that the new all-synchro four-speed was an immense improvement over the old Moss box in just about every way. No more first gear whine and just an easier drive through the gears overall. It would remain the mainstay of manual-transmissioned Jaguars, including the V-12 E-Types (which were still a half-dozen years away), for some years to come.

The 1965 redo was certainly the most significant updating the E-Type had yet received, but it still centered around the same two body styles—until 1966, when the line-up was expanded to include the 2+2.

Press shot of 4.2 Series I interior shows new seats with longer bottom cushions, thicker foam padding, and new pleated upholstery design. The seatbacks were now adjustable, as opposed to the earlier fixed-angle backs. *Jaguar Cars Archives*

No sooner was the production E-Type introduced in 1961 than Sir William began taking steps toward a roomier E-Type. According to a series of notes and memos between Bill Heynes and Lyons (reprinted virtually in full in Philip Porter's *Jaguar E-Type, The Definitive History*), the first mockup of what was to become the third E-Type body configuration was built in October of 1961. It contained "an additional 7 [inches] in the roof panel of the fixed head panel body only," Porter wrote, "with a view to providing occasional seats of a very limited nature to meet a demand which was then said to exist . . . it was thought at the time that the biggest market for a car of this type would be in the United States and

Below, factory press photograph of 4.2 fixed-head coupe. Note the whitewall tires, still a common sight on sports cars of the era, particularly British ones. Was there ever a purer automotive shape? *Jaguar Archives*

"Win on Sunday, sell on Monday" was a popular justification by auto makers for competition in the 1950s and 1960s. Jaguar, certainly knowing the benefit derived from its five Le Mans victories in the 1950s, attempted to shift some of the victorious "halo effect" to the E-Type. This particular E-Type was driven by Merle Brennan who, according to the advertisement, "won 29 SCCA road race and hill climb events out of 31 he entered."

would be for a vehicle that would compete with the Thunderbird."

The project would, strangely enough, be entitled the "XJ-8," though it was not an extension of the prior XJ series and no eight-cylinder engine option was even considered. There was also a good deal of controversy about exactly how the car should be expanded: just in length, or in width as well. The ever cost-conscious Lyons won out: the 2+2 measured 9 in longer, all of the increase coming between the wheels, with no increase in width or track. This translated to an increase in wheelbase from 96 to 105 in, and in increase in height, due to the continuance of the "sweep" of the roofline, of about 2 in. With an eye toward production and tooling expenses, Lyons also saw to it that approximately one-third of the panels were new (including much longer

doors), another third were modified pressings of existing panels, and the final third needed no changes at all. The increased interior volume was also helped by slightly reconfiguring the rear suspension tunnel.

Into the larger passenger compartment went two rather minuscule seats. The back portion of the seats, or squab, was mounted on a set of swinging brackets which allowed it to be moved forward when nobody was sitting in the back, greatly increasing rear luggage room. The glovebox acquired a lockable lid (on all models), and small package shelves appeared beneath the dash. In true "+2" fashion, the rear seat area was only adequate as occasional seating for adults, though preteens would be comfortable and travel in style. While full-sized adults would indeed fit, long-distance comfort was not a feature. A few of the Jaguar ads of the day attempted to capitalize on this "family sports car" adaptability, however, showing Mr., Mrs., and the kids out for a picnic. Another marketing philosophy capitalized on the added luggage space by showing a "Miss Jaguar Sports" toting beach toys, SCUBA gear, fishing poles, etc. Not exactly the image conjured up by the LeMans-winning D-Type, but whatever sells cars . . .

In Jaguar's own words: "In announcing this new addition to the highly successful E-Type range," it ran, "Jaguar has now extend their Grand Touring class of motoring to the man who, for business or pleasure, requires a car capable of accommodating four persons whilst retaining the standards of performance, braking and handling hitherto associated only with the finest of two seater models."

The longer wheelbase and reconfigured floor pan allowed Jaguar to offer another option—or concession—to U.S. drivers: an automatic transmission, the first in an E-Type. Jaguar offered a Borg Warner Model 8 three-speed automatic unit as an option on the 2+2 only; it would literally not fit in the coupe or roadster. Though previous Jaguar sedans had employed a BW Model 35, it was judged to be too old a design and not up to the torque output of the 4.2. The shift quadrant was mounted on the floor in place of the manual shifter. The Model 8 offered a "D2," which allowed start-off in second gear for icy conditions, and an "L" gear which allowed takeoff in first, or a manual downshift to second if the car

This particular 1967 Series I is from very late in the production run. Note that the headlights no longer sport the glass coverings of all prior models. These cars are often mistakenly identified as "Series I-1/2" models. This car maintains the pre-1968-specification interior and running gear, with no other major changes from the standard 1965–67 4.2s. The 1968 federalized models, the so-called "Series I-1/2 E-Types," are discussed in chapter four. *Author photo*

was traveling above about 25 mph. The quadrant and shift pattern were almost identical to the Ford C-4 automatic found in "America's version" of the E-Type 2+2, the Ford Mustang! The standard rear end ratio for automatic-equipped E-Types was 3.31:1, a bit taller than the standard 3.54:1 for manual cars. The 2+2 model was based at $700 more than a comparable coupe.

It's hard to improve on a masterpiece, and while few would call the 2+2 unattractive, stretching the original shape certainly did not improve on the original look. The windshield looked taller (it wasn't) and the previous flow of the fenderline was somewhat broken up by the long doors. The quick way to spot a 2+2 is to look for the chrome strip running down the door, just below the side windows. While the increase in leg

and head room was welcome, the added weight and the drop in performance that came with it were not. The 2+2 tipped the scales at about 200 lb more than a similarly equipped coupe, and 0–60 mph times were off by 0.7 sec for manual-equipped cars; an automatic 2+2 took approximately 2 sec more over a manual-equipped coupe to make the same run. Even the turning radius grew by about four feet, an effect of the longer wheelbase.

Contemporary road testers generally reacted well to the 2+2 and even the automatic transmission, though they clearly acknowledged a shift in purpose in exchange for a downward shift in performance. As *Autosport* commented, "In general, the transmission behaves well, though it is not as utterly smooth as some of the

Series I 4.2 specification engine was the last to carry triple sidedraft carbs and polished cam covers; neither would appear on the "federalized" Series II version. **Author photo**

sprung, it is more closely related to the Mark II and S-type in performance characteristic . . . Tall drivers in particular will find themselves better catered for in legroom and seating."

Perhaps the spiciest comment (and most politically incorrect) about the new E-Type came from the late *Road & Track* correspondent, Henry Manney. Manney had already dubbed the E-Type "The greatest crumpet collector known to man"— "crumpet" in this case meaning something along the lines of "young attractive person of the female persuasion." In a brief narrative about driving the new 2+2, Manney added: "As we've said before, the E-Type is the biggest value in the sports car market and with this variation takes a huge lead on the competition. And as for crumpet catching—as the front seats now recline into that extra room, a girl ain't safe no place, is she?"

So, in 4.2 form, the final iteration of the "pure" Series I, the E-Type had widened its appeal and marketability considerably. The model retained all the stylistic purity of the original design, yet added significant drivability improvements in the forms of an uprated engine, more comfortable interior, better brakes, tidier electrics, and a worlds-better manual transmission. The 2+2 body style and automatic transmission were there for those who wished those accouterments.

The best E-Types ever? I say yes.

more sophisticated American efforts . . . Though some power is absorbed by the transmission, the instantaneous up-changes on full throttle certainly add to the acceleration."

Autocar also liked the new model. "Brief acquaintance with an automatic 2+2 E-Type left several definite impressions," its reporter noted. "First, although it retains the performance of earlier manual E-Types it has quite a different atmosphere about it — a big cat without the bite, perhaps. Quieter, gentler, seemingly softer

The aluminum trim of the 3.8 models was nowhere to be found on the 4.2 cars; tinwork was replaced by leather-like vinyl, available in black only. This particular car carries a dealer-installed Motorola AM "Solid State" radio and aftermarket Selectaire air conditioning. **Author photo**

Rear aspect of the 4.2 was virtually unchanged from that of 3.8 Series I cars. *Author photo*

Though the E-Type never took home the big victories Jaguar had probably hoped for, it was popular among club racers of the day who could not afford Ferraris and didn't want to race Corvettes. This unidentified car and driver are seen competing in a local club race at Sebring, 1965. *Jim Spell photo; Jeff Herbert Collection*

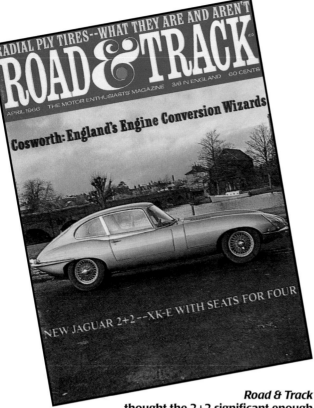

Road & Track thought the 2+2 significant enough to feature it on its April 1966 cover. The magazine also gave the car a favorable write-up in the issue's accompanying article.

A man, his car, and one of autodom's most popular rituals: the car wash (preferably on a warm Saturday afternoon, with a date planned for Saturday evening). This particular 1965 advertisement also advised that "if you're going to Europe, money-saving overseas delivery can be easily arranged."

Left, Jaguar's roster of great sporting cars was flush in the mid-to-late-1960s: marketed were the E-Type, the S-Type sedan, and the 420 sedan (all shown in this factory brochure), plus the still-popular Mk 2 sport sedan and the large Mk X, which by now had inherited the 4.2 E-Type's engine and was renamed the "420G."

Right, Jaguar assembly worker builds-up Series I engine; gold-painted head denotes it as being a higher compression model. *Jaguar Archives*

Jaguar publicity photo showing a most idyllic scene: red and black E-Types in the English countryside, picnic bas- kets at the ready. The stuff that dreams are made of. Note whitewall tires on the coupe. *Jaguar Archives*

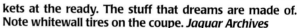

Jaguar's intent with the 2+2 was clear: appeal to families of more than two, and to women (top). The 4.2 interior detail shows automatic shift, hazard warning switch, and indicator light at lower left of dash, and binnacles beneath the dash (left). Rear seat area looks roomier than it is, though it's well suited to children and can accommodate adults in a pinch. Top portion of rear seat is hinged and folds forward, covering rear seats and increasing luggage capacity considerably. *Jaguar Cars Archives*

Right top and bottom, artwork from Series I 4.2 sales brochure. Interestingly enough, Jaguar elected to publish two different series of sales brochures upon the 4.2's introduction, one featuring the coupe and roadster only, and a separate one giving the specifications for all three but clearly highlighting the 2+2. Several monikers were applied to the 2+2, including "XKE Sedan" and, in this particular brochure, "2+2 Family Coupe."

Jaguar 4.2 XK-E Coupe, Roadster & 2+2 Family Coupe

"A different breed of cat"

Jaguar
4.2 XK-E Coupe & Roadster

"A different breed of cat"

It's not difficult to spot the 2+2's extra nine inches: doors are visibly longer; the roofline is higher; and the chrome strip is an easy identifier, though the effect is more noticeable from some angles than others. *Author photo*

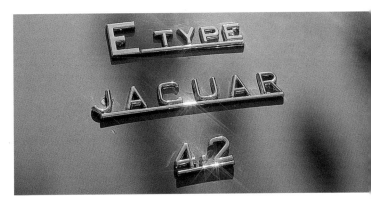

From the front angle, this 2+2 is nearly indistinguishable from a coupe. Additional bumper braces are aftermarket Amco pieces. *Author photo*

While the earlier cars were merely designated "Jaguar" on their rear decks, 4.2 models began proclaiming that they were in fact "E-Types," and also divulged the engine size. *Author photo*

An appropriate backdrop for such a properly British car: the most proper of British luxury liners, the Queen Mary, now in permanent residence at the Long Beach Harbor in Southern California. *Author photo.*

Automatic transmission gear selector looks natural enough in place of four-speed stick. Entry to the 2+2 is enhanced by larger doors and increased legroom. For exceptionally tall drivers, the 2+2 is about the only choice. *Author photo*

Right, E-Types posing on the production line in a rare factory color photo. These are Series I 4.2s. Since the primrose-yellow car in front is a 2+2, this photo would have been taken in 1966 or 1967. At this later stage of assembly, all three body styles were on the assembly line together. In upper right side of the photo, 3.8 S Sedan body shells can be seen on the high conveyer line. *Jaguar Daimler Heritage Trust*

JAGUAR
4

There is no such model as a 'Series I-1/2 E-Type.' No factory recognition is given to this designation.
—Karen Miller, Archivist, Jaguar Archives, Jaguar Cars

1968 Series "I-1/2"

So there you have it. Officially speaking, there are but three series of E-Types, only the first of which we have discussed thus far. There clearly *was*, however, a model with changes beyond those of the heretofore "pure" Series I cars, and it appeared prior to the introduction of the further-changed Series II models. The modifications, however, were not with the intent to improve the breed, nor did they come from the artistic hands of Jaguar's stylists, engineers, or senior management. They were essentially mandated by the U.S. Government, which was quickly making its way into the car business.

Though government regulations concerning the construction, certification, and testing of automobiles were nothing new, Congress stepped up its involvement by passing comprehensive new legislation to be effective for the 1968 model year. The primary targets were safety issues and allowable levels of exhaust emission pollutants. This era really signaled the beginning of "automotive design by mandate" that is, of course, very

From the outside, it's difficult to tell a 1968 "Series I-1/2" car from a late-1967. Headlights no longer wear glass covers, but all the bumper and lighting hardware is virtually pure Series I. Notice that the wheel configuration has evolved to the "flat" hub surface and the previously eared knock-off spinner is now in the "safety" version that must be removed with a special wrench. *David W. Newhardt photo*

1968 4.2 "Series I-1/2" Fixed-Head Coupe. *David W. Newhardt photo*

much with us today, though somehow the idea of a propane-powered 1995 E-Type with air bags in the doors doesn't seem very appealing . . .

With America being Jaguar's most important E-Type market, the engineers at Browns Lane had little choice but to make the car comply with U.S. regulations. One estimate places the cost of developing or modifying hardware to bring the E-Type into compliance at approximately $500,000—a considerable sum in the mid-1960s, though probably less than it would cost General Motors to tool up for a new taillight today.

According to documentation provided by Jaguar, the transformation of the E-Type from "pure" Series I 1967 cars to fully federalized Series II 1969 models involved two intermediate steps: the first really quite minor (though certainly visible); the second much more significant. One was a series of changes to U.S. and Canadian E-Types that took place early in the 1967 model year. The main differences, from an appearance standpoint, were a redesigned wire wheel and the elimination of the glass headlight covers. The hub portion of the wheel, which previously contained something of a rib, was now a flatter piece of metal, though it retained the two-eared knock-off spinner of the early cars. These were the only significant changes to what we can colloquially dub the first of the "I-1/2" Series cars, though they were really just late-year 1967 models.

Twin Zenith-Stromberg 175 CD-2 carburetors replace previous triple SU setup. "Jaguar" emblem cast into passenger-side valve cover. Enthusiasts seem to be split on the newer cam cover design, some preferring the "clas- sic" look and easy-to-polish smooth aluminum surface, others preferring the ribbed surface as being more technically interesting. *David W. Newhardt photo*

1968 brought major changes to the engine compartment. New crinkle-finish black cam covers replace previously smooth, polished units, and aluminum heat exchanger carries heat from exhaust manifolds to carbs for quicker warmup and fewer cold-start emissions. Twin fan design is now in place, but one carb (as compared to Series I cars) is missing! *David W. Newhardt photo*

The second group of cars that could be called "Series I-1/2s" are the 1968 model year E-Types, which retained the look of the cars described above, but carried substantial hardware changes inside the car and under the hood.

Most expensive, and most difficult, of the new laws to meet were those concerning emissions. Though the bore and stroke of the 4.2 XK engine did not change (as it had previously in its redesign from the 3.8-ltr version), the intake manifolding and carburetion were completely

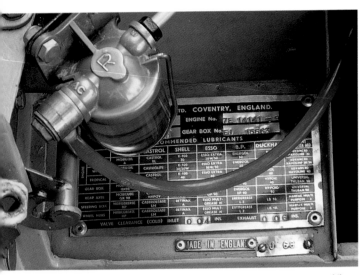

Detailed number plate gives all lubrication specifications for the XK engine, as well as serial, engine, chassis, and transmission ID numbers for the entire car. The glass bowl contains a replaceable fuel filter element. *David W. Newhardt photo*

replaced. Gone were the triple sidedraft SUs; in their place were now *two* Zenith-Stromberg CD2SE units. Though fuel injection was considered (Jaguar had been researching the development of an FI systems since the mid-1950s), the science was not yet developed enough to where a cost-effective system would meet both performance and emission goals. Mercedes was about the only manufacturer employing fuel injection at the time, and the Bosch systems they used were both complicated and expensive. Hence, the Strombergs, developed with emission compliance in mind.

An elaborate, aluminum-cast crossover manifold was developed to channel the gas/air mixture to another area of the engine for pre-

Below, 1968 4.2 "Series I-1/2" Fixed-Head Coupe rear luggage compartment. *David W. Newhardt photo*

Factory photo of fully federalized 1968 E-Type roadster.
Jaguar Cars Archives

heating to ensure more efficient combustion. While the additional hardware, along with many, many other detail changes, did allow the engine to meet the new requirements, the extra machinery and increased engine heat could do nothing but decrease the engine's output.

Rated outputs changed as follows:

	Federalized 4.2	Series I 4.2
Horsepower @ RPM	246 @ 5,500	265 @ 5,400
Torque @ RPM	263 @ 4,000	283 @ 4,000

Another instant visual tipoff of the federalized 4.2 was that the previously polished cam covers were replaced by a new design, the main surface of which was finished in black "crinkle" paint, with raised ribs (or cooling fins) down the middle that were left with a natural aluminum look. A Jaguar badge was an add-on piece to these new-look cam covers.

When coupled to an average weight increase of approximately 150 pounds (depending upon body configuration), performance suffered. This was not as damaging as it may initially sound;

E-Types on the Silver Screen

Today, auto manufacturers and public relations firms work *very* hard to place their products in movies and on television. With advertising that can run into the hundreds of thousands of dollars for even one minute, the concept of having one's product on screen for hours—for almost no cost—is a car maker's dream. While product placement wasn't always such big business, the notion that a starring role can often transform brand recognition overnight is nothing new. Just ask Aston Martin about the ripple effect it enjoyed after the James Bond flick *Goldfinger.* People still identify 007 with that whiz-bang DB5—thirty years later.

E-Types have appeared in many movies, sometimes in minor roles and occasionally as main characters. One campy car cult flick featuring two E-Types is *The Italian Job.* The movie opens with a Lamborghini Miura winding its way through the Italian countryside. Its driver, it seems, has gotten on the bad side of the Mob, as he and the Miura have an unfortunate encounter with a skip loader at the end of a tunnel. One exotic car destroyed, and we've barely finished the credits! The E-Types are both Series Is, a black coupe and a red 1961 roadster (the roadster quite unique in being only the twelfth open-air E-Type built). The handsome pair are part of bank robber extraordinaire Michael Caine's all-British stable, which also includes an Aston DB-4 drophead and three specially prepared Minis. The Minis are an integral part of the getaway plan for knocking off an armored truck in downtown Turin.

The E-Types never make it that far; they and the Aston meet up with the same tribe of Mafioso that put an end to the Lambo in the opening scene, on presumably the same road. The Mafia king now deems it appropriate to reinforce the notion of just who is boss to the brash foreign thief. You guessed it: the same tractor chugs its way over to the black coupe, its hydraulic shovel handily wasting the roof and a majority of the rest of the bodywork. Caine spits a few remarks at The Don. The Italian apparently doesn't feel the Englishman gets the point, so he commands the skip to administer the same treatment to the red roadster. Appropriately enough, its license plate reads "848 CRY." The Aston gets the worst of it though; after a thorough thrashing, it gets sent over a cliff, a fate that had awaited the three hapless Minis as well. 848 CRY survives. It's since been beautifully restored, but the rest are most likely long gone. Like we said, this was a cult flick.

52 Pick-Up stars Roy Scheider, Ann-Margaret, and a very handsome silver-blue Series I roadster. This slick, early-1980s film pits Scheider as a successful, self-made man against three seriously sleazy goons who videotape him cavorting about with a lovely blonde woman about half his age. Scheider will have none of their extortion plot, so the head goon goes on a killing spree and kidnaps Ann-Margaret, Scheider's loyal and attractive wife.

The E-Type shows up in the very first scene, as Scheider carefully removes the hardtop in his garage. Head Goon throws an eye on the car early on, coyly asking Scheider, "You restored it yourself, didn't you?" Another great scene shows Scheider dutifully tuning the engine while a scared and frustrated Ann-Margaret fumes: "I hope you know what you can do with those plugs when you get 'em out!"

The movie was directed by John Frankenheimer *(Grand Prix),* so well-done car scenes are to be expected. In one such sequence, Scheider has just learned that his lady friend has been done in by the bad trio, and he goes for a drive to clear his thoughts. He whips the E-Type down some lovely mountain roads at sunset, and the sound effects are quite authentic. There's also some worthwhile in-car and car-to-car footage.

Scheider appears to be giving in to the extortion plan in exchange for the safe return of his wife, and the E-Type plays an integral role in the movie's final scene. The bad guy agrees to take the E-Type as part of the payoff, after first asking if it's a six or a V-12. A somewhat startled Scheider ardently replies, "It's a six!" The two meet on a bridge in Long Beach, where a drugged but living Ann-Margaret is exchanged for a bag of money and the E-Type. As soon as Mr. Bad fires the engine and turns on the stereo, the now-rigged E-Type locks him inside, plays a brief strain of "Stars and Stripes Forever"—and then violently explodes. A close look at the tape in slow motion reveals that the cherry roadster was swapped for a hulking—but real—E-Type just prior to the big bang.

Warner Brothers' *Gumball Rally* may be one of the greatest—if not, certainly the most humorous—automotive spoof films ever. Basically a takeoff on the Cannonball Baker Sea-to-Shining Sea cross country marathons, *Gumball* assembles an amazing array of cars and characters. The Ferrari Daytona Spyder and 427 Cobra driven by Raul Julia and Michael Sarazan are real ones, and a scene involving the two of them splashing down the Los Angeles River Canal is priceless.

The movie pokes a lot of fun at a lot of things, not the least of which is a hapless red V-12 roadster that refuses to start. In the beginning, its starter whirs enthusiastically. The action flashes back to the same car and its luckless pilots every fifteen minutes or so, the starter getting weaker and weaker each time. In one scene, the two are working under the car as one comments, "It's a handsome design." Decidedly miffed, the other replies, "I wish it *ran*." It's a fun flick, and much more worthwhile than the Burt Reynolds *Cannonball Run* pictures that would follow.

Other American films with notable E-Type appearances include *Brannigan*, *Silver Streak*, and *The Blues Brothers* (in which the E-Type is driven by a lovely and properly accented Twiggy). It's just too bad "Q" did not see fit to field-equip Commander Bond with an E-Type: it would have made *Goldfinger* just that much better.

remember that any manufacturer selling in the United States had the same obstacles to contend with, and just about everyone's acceleration numbers were off compared to those achieved with prior, non-smog-equipped hardware. (We'll discuss more about performance and contemporary comparisons in the next chapter, which deals with the Series II cars.)

The other major changes wrought by federal compliance were to be found in the interior, and again, few of the modifications could truly be classed as improvements. A redesigned instrument panel did away with the neat rows of toggle switches, replacing them with black plastic rocker switches. A traffic/hazard warning light system was also incorporated, but if there was any change that stole a bit of the E-Type's British charm, it was the disappearance of one button from the center dashboard: the separate starter button, a bit of an old-world Jaguar trademark, gave way to an integral ignition/starter keylock. The clock, previously a small unit mounted within the tachometer, was replaced by a standard gauge-sized unit, and it filled the spot on the dash previously occupied by headlight controls. All in the name of safety . . .

A few of the changes were difficult to spot, or really were of no consequence: the addition of a collapsible steering column; a breakaway rear view mirror; some additional padding, etc.

Many books claim that these so-called Series I-1/2 models are mongrels that were assembled with whatever bits were left around the works, or as new pieces were brought on line. Again, according to Jaguar and materials provided by JCNA, this is not quite true. To quote from the introduction of an eighty-plus page technical manual presented at the JCNA national convention in 1994 (a copy of which may be purchased; see Appendix): "No internal or external publications, or chassis records use the term 'Series I-1/2.' Similarly, the designation 'Series I-1/2' does not appear in any official factory materials. It was, and is, an artificial term applied by the public to those 4.2 "E" types [sic] which were fitted in stages with Federally mandated safety and emissions components."

Moreover, I've seen enthusiasts, car owners, and concours judges engaged in heated discussions about whether a particular component is correct for a car of this era, or about whether the late-1967 "open headlight" cars are considered "I-1/2 cars" or not. It matters little. Though these 1968 cars were clearly transitional models, and though there are undoubtedly a few cars extant that may contradict the exact manner in which the federal changes were rolled out, the moral of the story is that they are still E-Types in every sense of the word, and no less should be thought or made of them. Unfortunately, tougher times were yet to come.

OUCH! E-Type undergoing crash testing at the Motor Industry Research Center. This car is believed to be a 1968 2+2, but it's difficult to tell as neither interior nor engine compartment can be seen. The car is fitted with Series I knock-off nuts, but as they could be inter-changed on this mule car, this is not a guarantee of its being an earlier or later car. The car also carries its door locks in the door skin, not in the lock, indicating a 1968-specification car or at least a car fitted with 1968 doors. *Jaguar Daimler Heritage Trust*

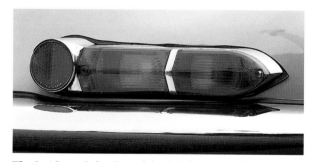

The last hurrah for the original, dainty, and slim rear tail-light treatment. A new, federalized, not-nearly-as-attractive below-bumper design would debut in 1969. Interestingly enough, the taillight housings for coupe and convertible models are not interchangeable, each being slightly different to accommodate the contours of each body style's fender shape. *David W. Newhardt photo*

Jaguar designs have maintained a certain feline character due to the gentle inward tapering of the rear fenders. This same effect can be seen on the XJ6, 3.8 S-Type, and Mark 10. Jaguar borrowed a styling effect and cooling aid from the hot rod idiom, punching two rows of louvers into the head just above the engine. *David W. Newhardt photo*

Changes abound in the interior, most noticeably the "switch of the switches" from the previous toggle units to new safety-inspired rocker switch units. The ignition key and starter button become one and move to the steering column, while the small clock previously found in the tachometer is enlarged and makes its way to the center instrument facia. Note new recessed latches on doors. *David W. Newhardt photo*

Left, tachometer no longer bears dainty clock at the bottom, and instrument surrounds are now finished in non-glare black rather than the previous chrome bezzles. Hazard/flasher warning light moves from its previous add-on position at the lower left of the dash to a more permanent-looking spot between the two main gauges. Fortunately, the classic steering wheel remains. *David W. Newhardt photo*

Custom E-Types: Not Leaving Well Enough Alone

Few would argue that the E-Type was, and is, one of the purest automotive shapes ever to make production. An exercise in design harmony, its elements were blended and balanced to achieve a look that is rare in its timelessness. This is especially true in the case of the Series I cars, the E-Type in its most original form. Not only Jaguar, through its own design studies and prototypes, but many noted stylists and styling houses attempted to improve on the original, using the E-Type as a basis for their creativity. In short, some of their efforts yielded attractive automobiles; most did not. A few of the more notable efforts follow.

Frua E-Type

Frua is among the best known of Italian design houses, and it once attempted to graft some of its signature styling cues onto the E-Type. This car, commissioned by British Jaguar dealer John Combs, began life as a standard 1965 Series I coupe. Frua's treatment was focused primarily on the end caps. The new nose carried bits of Maserati Mistral (another Frua design) and maybe a touch of Alfa Romeo Duetto in the center grille area. A small scoop was cut into the front of the hood, and some tacky chrome grillework was added to the engine cooling vents. The rear treatment encased the taillights in a large chrome bumper fixture. Surprisingly enough, this look bears a striking resemblance to the yet-to-come Series III's rear aspect. Virtually everything between the bumpers was standard fare, and while this particular car didn't look bad, it would be difficult to call it an improvement over the original.

Raymond Loewy E-Type

Raymond Loewy's portfolio of industrial design work has been well documented, from the Shell Oil logo to several vehicles for Studebaker. Loewy also began with a Series I coupe, and the look mixes Italian, English, and, strangely enough, Japanese styling cues. The front end was shortened approximately 10 in, and a sort of Ferrariesque grille shape (minus the egg crate) was fashioned in. The plexiglass-enclosed quad headlights don't look half bad, and Loewy also carved a scoop into the front of the hood. The rear treatment employed simple round taillights and a refashioned license plate nacelle. The rear window line/C-pillar treatment is reminiscent of both the Toyota 2000 and the Datsun 240Z, cars that would come only after the Loewy E-Type's construction in 1966; the treatment works quite well with the natural bulge of the factory rear fender line. Overall length was decreased nearly 15 in. The coachwork was handled by Pinchon-Parat in France, and while the look is certainly aggressive, it would again be hard to say it's better than that of a standard Series I.

Bertone Pirana

Another well-known Italian styling house brought in to design a prototype of the E-Type was Bertone. While the Frua project was essentially limited to a facelift of the original coachwork, the Pirana was a complete rebody. England's *Daily Telegraph Magazine* commissioned Nuccio Bertone to create an "ideal dream car," the project being essentially a publicity stunt for the magazine. This is the type of project that could have only been successful in the 1960s; imagine today's cost of a magazine or newspaper hiring any one of the major styling concerns to create a one-off show car, just for the news value!

The project began life as a 2+2 chassis to which Bertone affixed truly handsome fastback coupe coachwork. Pirana's shape is largely the work of Marcello Gandini, who would go on to design the Countach and Diablo, among other significant Italian exotica. The Pirana design, especially from the front or in direct profile, is a clear predecessor to the Lamborghini Espada. No coincidence to be sure, as Bertone also penned the Espada, and in truth, the Pirana may be the better looking of the two.

Several British manufacturers contributed to the project, including Connolly, Lucas, Triplex, and Britax. Inside, some E-Type cues remain, though the builders packed in as much electronic gear as they could, including power windows, antenna, a special stereo with tape recorder, air temperature gauge, and even a device allowing the driver to check the engine oil level—from the driver's seat! Commonplace for today's computer-managed automobiles, but quite heady stuff for 1967.

The Pirana made the rounds on the international show car circuit, including London, Turin, Montreal, and New York, before being sold to a private party. To this writer's eye, it is far and away the most professionally conceived and executed (not to mention handsome) E-Type concept exercise.

Guyson E12

Another notable, if not quite tasteful, interpretation of the E-Type theme was the Guyson E12. Guyson was a British industrial firm, its managing director being one Jim Thompson. Thompson wrecked his Series III roadster and engaged Aston Martin designer William Towns to recreate it as his own special machine. The result was an exceptionally long, slab-sided roadster. The blacked-out rocker sills and lower body cladding only served to visually lengthen the car, and the nose was virtually without a grille. Surface detail was practically nonexistent. The look is so typically 1970s, right down to the deep-dish alloy wheels and whitewall tires. The car was built in 1974.

Guyson was attempting to fashion the fiberglass panels so they could be easily installed and removed, allowing the owner to convert and reconvert the car with little effort. Mr. Towns was apparently pleased with his efforts, as he too converted a V-12 E-Type to the Guyson bodywork. The scheme went no further, and only these two cars were built. While considered eye-catching by many at the time, the Guyson E12 looks flat and out of proportion today. It must have caught someone's eye, as Mr. Towns was able to redeploy the same flavor a few years later, on the Aston Martin Lagonda sedan.

Pininfarina Jaguar XJ Spider

This particular concept car is not based on an actual E-Type. In fact, it came along nearly five years after E-Type production ended. Why it is worthy of mention is the fact that the E-Type look was still a worthy target. It is not uncommon for styling houses to build concept vehicles "on spec" in the hopes that a manufacturer will pick up the design for a production model. Italy's Pininfarina attempted just that with the XJ Spider in 1978. The basis for the Spider was actually an XJ-S, and the evolutionary styling ties to the E-Type—and the XJ-13 mid-engined prototype—are undeniable. The E-Type's rounded nose integrates nicely with hidden headlights and a cowl shape reminiscent of the Ferrari Daytona. The interior richly melds stock Jaguar controls and futuristic digital instrumentation with a decidedly Italian-looking upholstery treatment. Pininfarina's Leonardo Fioravanti was largely responsible for the look, and it is simply stunning.

The V-12 engine was retained, and the Spider was a runner, unlike many such concept studies. Had Jaguar elected to redesign the E-Type for production into the mid-1970s and early 1980s, it could have done little better than did Pininfarina with the XJ Spider.

In spite of all these efforts, however, the E-Type is one shape that such individualized exercises may *never* improve upon.

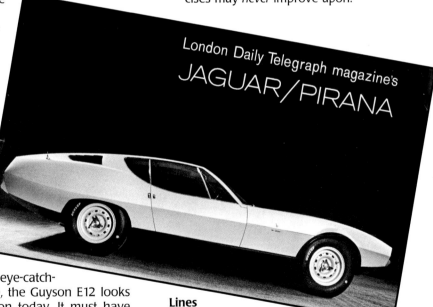

London Daily Telegraph magazine's JAGUAR/PIRANA

Lines from the Bertone-styled Jaguar/Pirana were clearly borrowed for use on the Lamborghini Espada, which was on the drawing board as the Pirana debuted. The longish nose and engine compartment suited both Jaguar's XK six and Lamboghini's large, four-cam V-12. This photograph was taken from what appeared to be a sales and public relations brochure.

JAGUAR 5

*All you Faithful Readers still holding your
breath for the V-12 Jaguar XK-F may exhale.
It simply isn't time yet.*
—Car and Driver *May 1969*

1969–1970 Series II 4.2

As the time came to deliver fully federalized
1969 production models, the Jaguar brain trust
was faced with several factors that, depending
upon which direction the company elected to
take the E-Type, would change the car's develop-
mental pattern significantly. Not only did the car
have to deal with the emissions and safety
requirements ordered by the U.S. Government,
but other challenges were offered by the
exotic/sports car market itself.

When the E-Type was introduced at the
dawn of the 1960s, it was genuinely quite
advanced from a technical standpoint, or at least
it offered design features found only on much
more expensive cars. But the cutting edge of
sports car design continued to follow a new direction as the decade progressed: *mid-engined*
machines. The diminutive DeTomaso Vallelunga
began the trend in about 1965, but was only
available in very limited production. Yet by 1968,
when the "Series I-1/2" began the E-Type's transformation toward fully federalized Series II models, there were several mid-engined models
either available or about to be introduced: the

**Rear plinth mounts new taillight units (an outside part
from Lucas, also shared with other cars), and twin backup lights replace the previous single unit. Neither looks
better than the previous designs, though the beefier
rear bumper provides better protection than the dain-
tier Series I split bumpers. *Author photo***

The big news of this display, at the New York Hilton ball-room in 1968, was the new XJ6 sedan, though the 1969 Series II E-Types were also on hand. Two questions come to mind: Why is there no 2+2 to be seen (at least within the range of this photo) and why is the crowd so sparse? This could have been a more private showing for dealers or the media, as opposed to the normally crowded general public introduction. *Jaguar Archives*

Lamborghini Miura; the Ferrari 246 Dino; and the DeTomaso Mangusta, to name a few.

There was also a good bit of new competition in the front-engined ranks, including the Ferrari Daytona, Maserati Ghibli, and, most significant given the E-Type's price class, a new-for-1968 Corvette. Competition also came from new six-cylinder cars like the BMW 2800 CS and even Leyland's own Triumph TR6. Life was not to get any easier for the E-Type.

With the XJ13, Jaguar proved it could indeed engineer mid-engined cars, but the E-Type had not yet run its full course. Bill Heynes, Malcom Sayer, and their respective minions did experiment with a more "modern" version of the E-Type. These projects, called "XJ21," "XJ22,"
and "XJ23," lived only on the drawing boards or as clay mockups. Oliver Winterbottom, a member of the Jaguar styling staff, built a rather handsome mockup for the XJ21 concept, which appeared as somewhat a cross between an Aston Martin DBS coupe and an Iso Grifo (especially from the rear).

In the end, however, Jaguar stuck to the original E-Type. The reasons were most likely an amalgamation of economics, the absorption of Jaguar into the British Leyland fold, and Jaguar's reluctance to give up on a design that sold well and was "only" seven years old at the time (the typical product cycle for Sir William's cars ran about ten years). All three body configurations were retained.

As noted, some of the changes necessary to meet U.S. requirements were incorporated into the 1968 models, and the balance would come along with the 1969s. The headlights, which already gave up their glass covers, now appeared more pronounced by having been moved forward approximately two inches. They also received larger chrome bezels, and the now-larger turn signal/running lights were moved down below the bumper. Additional marker lights sprouted from the side of the front fenders, and the bumper was now a thicker, one-piece unit.

In order to make room for the air conditioning heat exchanger, the radiator opening was in-creased by some 68 percent, which certainly did increase the airflow substantially. This may have also aided engine cooling, which was always marginal on the earlier cars, though the actual air inlet to the radiator did not in-crease. Additional cooling modifications included a cross-flow radiator of increased capacity, and twin, thermostatically controlled electric fans replaced the previous single unit. These improvements to the E-Type's cooling capacity were more necessary than ever, and the car's increasing weight and pollution controls mandated it. Additionally, and for the first time, an Adwest power steering system was an available option, and air conditioning was ordered more and more often, especially by U.S. buyers.

Price P.O.E. East Coast, slightly higher Gulf and West ports.

Why wait?

The Jaguar XKE has 15 standard features Detroit is considering for its cars of the future. At $5534, what are you waiting for? **Jaguar**

Whereas many previous adver-tisements "grocery-listed" the E-Type's specifications and technical sophistication, by the late-1960s, the ads began to take on a much more cerebral style. This par-ticular ad invokes an undeniable sex appeal and only cursorily mentions the "15 standard features Detroit is considering for its cars of the future." The East Coast price for this Series II roadster: still an unbelievably rea-sonable $5,534.

1969 E-Type Series II Roadster. *Author photo*

Trunk ID on 1969 E-Type Series II Roadster. *Author photo*

Series II wire wheel carrying federal safety specification "earless" spinner. No longer could E-Type owners employ the traditional bronze and rawhide mallet; a special wrench now replaced it in the factory-supplied tool roll. "Red line" tires were a very popular period addition to this 1969 E-Type. *Author photo*

Other mechanical changes included Girling brake discs and larger-capacity calipers.

Revised lighting requirements also altered the rear aspect of the E-Type. The previous slim, twin bumperettes again gave way to a more substantial single-piece unit with overriders; side marker lights were now tacked onto the sides of the rear fenders. A stainless steel plinth, mounted below the new rear bumper, served as the mounting surface for larger taillights—the

same Lucas units found on certain Lotus models. Twin backup lights also hung from the bumper. In addition, the metal fixture carried the license plate, as the previously indented rear panel was now covered up. Reconfiguration of the exhaust system was also required. All in all, the new hardware did the job and was relatively inexpensive to develop, but nobody would say it was a stylistic improvement in any way.

Among the easy-to-spot detail changes were adjustable headrests. The previous two-eared knock-off hub gave way to a hub of the non-eared variety that required a special wrench to remove. Like the aforementioned starter button, the

The 1969–70 2+2 carries the same front and rear treatments as other Series IIs, as well as a new, more steeply raked windshield. The windshield's base was moved forward toward the front of the car, de-emphasizing the upright look of the previous Series I 2+2. The overall look is a considerable improvement. *Jaguar Archives*

bronze-and-leather mallet used to remove a knock-off wire wheel was no longer to be found in the E-Type's tool bag. Things, indeed, *had changed.* For the first time, a stamped steel, chrome finished "turbo disc" wheel (from the new XJ6) was offered—as an option! This wheel, which also was to appear on many Jaguar sedans, later item became standard equipment on the E-Type, with wire wheels now the option—a unique twist of marketing, and a reflection on the ever-changing tastes of the buying public. The limited-slip differential, also previously standard on all but the 2+2, became an extra cost.

Though purists may find this difficult to swallow now, the 2+2 had become the best selling E-Type model, and it received a somewhat major modification of its own during the transformation to Series II specification. When the Series I coupe was quite literally stretched into the 2+2 configuration, the windshield and its installed angle were not changed. The slope of the longer roofline, combined with the larger doors and side glass, made the windshield appear quite upright. This was remedied on the Series II, as the base of the wind-

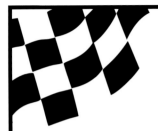

The E-Type and Historic Racing–
Past and Present

By Patrick C. Paternie

Where does one draw the line when discussing the XK-E as a vintage racer?

Lou Fidanza was racing old E-Types long before they were considered vintage race cars. Fidanza, owner of Gran Turismo Jaguar in Perry, Ohio, and his driver, Freddy Baker, campaigned a sixteen-year-old XK-E to a national championship in the 1980 SCCA runoffs at Road Atlanta. The team beat a host of factory-backed efforts, including Bob Sharp's Datsun ZX, driven by the 1979 C-Production champion, Paul Newman.

On the way to victory, the white #19 Jaguar became the first sports car to turn a lap at over 100mph on the twisty Georgia circuit. It was also the first non-factory car in C-Production history to capture the pole and the first to win the class championship. Recall that at the time C-Production was the SCCA's premier class for sports cars, where manufacturers like Datsun, Triumph, Mazda, and Porsche all battled for wins on Sunday to sell cars on Monday.

The 1982 season brought the curtain down on the XK-powered #19. Now racing in GT1 with the big-bore V-8-powered sports cars and sedans like Corvettes and Camaros, the car's last hurrah was a convincing twenty second victory over Newman's powerful 280 ZX turbo at Mid-Ohio. Not a bad exit for an aged race car that had been in competition since 1973, the year before Jaguar ceased production of the E-Type.

Fidanza, whose company develops and sells high-performance Jaguar parts, continues to be involved with racing E-Types. In June 1988 he brought out a "new" #19, a red 1966 roadster, which was driven by Tim Dunn to victory in the Andrew Whyte Memorial Race at Mid-Ohio. This first "all Jaguar" race in North America was held in honor of the noted Jaguar historian and author, who had passed away a month earlier. Twenty classic Jaguars competed in an event dominated by Dunn and his red E-Type.

Presently, Fidanza and his crew at Gran Turismo Jaguar are in the final phase of constructing a detailed replica of the V-12 E-Type raced by Group 44 (the original resides at Browns Lane). While striving to maintain authenticity, Fidanza points out that state-of-the-art technology is being applied in the construction process as much as possible. He does admit that the high caliber of engineering originally performed by Group 44 leaves little room for improvement.

An interesting historical footnote is that the engine in the car is an original Huffaker V-12, capable of an estimated 490 hp. Although jointly backed by Jaguar to develop the V-12 E-Type, Group 44 on the East Coast and Huffaker on the West Coast worked independently of each other and became rivals on the race track. Twenty years later, thanks to an odd twist of fate and Lou Fidanza, the stronger of the two engines has been mated with the stronger of the two chassis. Could this hybrid be the ultimate E-Type racer?

Right now, one of the hottest E-Types in vintage racing is the 1963 XK-E coupe owned and driven by Bernard Juchli of Los Gatos, California. A consistent overall winner in B-Production (a class populated by Shelbys and Corvettes) for the last three years, the car was originally a club racer in England. Juchli brought it to the U.S. in 1984 and completed a thorough restoration before heading for the track. The immaculate racer is as beautiful as it is potent, finished off in the traditional Lister colors of green and yellow.

The powerplant is a 3.8-ltr six that delivers 330 hp. It willingly revs to 7,000 rpm, although Juchli prefers to shift at 6,500 rpm. He admits to seeing the tach needle hit 7,200 on a blast down the long straight at Seattle, which he reckons to be worth about 150mph. Shifting is accomplished with a 1965 vintage all-synchro gearbox. This unit supplants the original Moss box in def-

Bernard Juchli's E-Type historic racer reveals a few Lightweight racer cues, but wears a color and paint scheme more often seen on late-1950s Lister-Jaguars. Historic-racing an E-Type is rewarding, but expensive. *Bob Dunsmore photo*

erence to a scarcity of replacement parts for the latter and the non-synchro first gear.

The car also sports stiffened springs and torsion bars, along with Dunlop pin drive alloy wheels. Lightweight parts include an aluminum hood, doors, and rear hatch. The car is immaculately turned out, a tribute to Juchli's passion for the marque and the restoration shop he has run since 1981.

Thinking of vintage-racing an E-Type? Plan on spending around $30–40,000 for a good mid-level racer, according to Jason Len of XKs Unlimited in San Luis Obispo, California. Len's company has over twenty years of experience restoring and building high-performance Jaguars for customers around the world. His estimate assumes that you already own a solid car and are interested in reliability and low maintenance, as opposed to owning an all-out track burner.

Start with a 1962–67 E-Type and drop in the 3.8-ltr motor. This will not only ensure eligibility for most vintage racing or-ganizations, but it's the best setup for anyone on a budget where reliability is more important than maximum horsepower. Racers watching their budget are also watching their tachometers. Stay below 5,500 rpm and Len says you can go with stock rods, a stock 4.2 oil pump, a lightened stock flywheel, stock valves, distributor, clutch, gearbox, and limited slip differential. Even the stock wire wheels will do for a mildly tuned car.

continued on next page

Quality forged pistons are a must. A 9.5–10.5:1 compression ratio gives maximum reliability, while those who get a thrill powering out of the turns will want to squeeze out 11 or 12:1. The stock HD-8 SU carburetors work best for most cars.

Cooling is the early E-Type's weak point. Len suggests that the bigger the radiator, the better. The radiator should be well ducted and sealed to the hood. An oil cooler is also strongly recommended.

The stock 3.8 gearbox is strong but very slow shifting. Len prefers the 1965–67 4.2 gearbox for its better synchros, oil pump, and close ratio gearset. He says you can spot the close ratio gears by the small groove machined around their faces. A triple-disc racing clutch is very expensive but will last forever, while giving superior acceleration. Rear end gearing depends on the race track, but anywhere from 3:54 to 4:55 is suitable.

Carbon pads and massive cooling ducts are necessities if club rules only allow the stock brakes; otherwise, retrofit Series II or III brakes.

Basic suspension modifications would include Koni shocks and heavy-duty sway bars. Next up would be heavier torsion bars for the front and heim-jointed trailing arms at the rear. Triangulated trailing arms and solid mounts for the rear suspension would be the next rung on the ladder for those with bigger budgets.

The most common wheel size is 15x6 in. Series III wires are the preferred wheels for those who want the vintage look. Mini-lites with wire wheel splines are also an option. By bolting on hubs from a sedan, you can fit various alloy wheels. Tire choice depends on club restrictions.

It should go without saying that proper safety equipment, like roll bars or roll cages, fuel cells, fire systems, and safety belts, will be properly installed and maintained.

"After that, the sky's the limit," Len says. "How fast do you want to go?"

Lou Fidanza feels that about $125,000 will build an E-Type racer that will reach the stratosphere in appearance and performance.

Racing a vintage E-Type is obviously not for the faint of pocketbook. This may account for the big cats being on vintage racing's endangered species list. The above examples, however, should prove that owning one of these ferocious felines can be a very rewarding experience.

shield was moved forward several inches, to just behind the rear hood line. The change increased the rake of the windshield and smoothed the look of the 2+2, especially in profile. A bit of the original coupe's sleekness was regained.

It should not be ignored that British Leyland and Jaguar's marketing folks were also aiming the Series II E-Type at what may have seemed like an unlikely target in the 1960s: women. In the Swinging Sixties, high-performance sports cars were still largely the dominion of males. Jaguar's shift in marketing can be seen in the fact that a 2+2 could be ordered with an automatic transmission, factory-installed air conditioning, whitewall tires, and power steering. Perhaps Jaguar thought this combination was just the ticket for a woman of means and sporting desire, though from a performance and styling standpoint, it was a vastly different breed of cat (pun intended) than a Series I roadster.

The specifications of the federalized 4.2 XK engine were discussed in the last chapter, though given reductions in both torque and horsepower of approximately 7 percent, it's no surprise that performance, in just about every category, decreased. Added weight due to additional equipment and power losses on AC and/or power steering-equipped cars took their toll as well. The E-Type was still in the game, however, as other manufacturers had to contend with the same restrictions, so the playing field was still essentially level.

Car and Driver tested a '69 model roadster and gave it a warm reception, pointing out not only the changes mandated by law, but many of the refinements made to the car's benefit along the way. "Even if you're an automotive fire-in-the-guts, change-for-the-sake-of-change revolutionist you'll have to admit that that's what the

Polished alloy crossover manifold carries heat from rear exhaust manifold to carburetors for quicker warmup and fewer "cold start" emissions. Credit must be given to Jaguar for attempting to come up with a handsome, nicely finished piece to accomplish this; many American cars employed cheap-looking, painted, stamped steel pieces or flimsy-looking, metalized hoses for this type of hardware. Old-fashioned acorn nuts for head and cam covers look just right with new black finish. *Jaguar Daimler Heritage Trust*

Jaguar people have still got (a winning horse) with the XK-E. They had one from the moment they unwrapped the first brakeless, over-heating, Shelby Cobra-like, roughneck production model in 1962, and they've got one with the well-manicured, smooth operating, slicked down version we're talking about today." *C&D* pinpointed one aspect of the new engine's performance that was significant to the American driver, however, and that was the fact that while the peak torque had decreased, the rpm at which it was achieved had also decreased: ". . . performance up to U.S. speed limits is actually improved over the 1968 triple carburetor

setup . . . quarter mile times have been reduced from 15.6 sec to 15.3 at 90 mph," it noted. "In addition, the engine revisions have lowered the torque curve into a far more usable area, which means you can prowl away in top gear from 1,500 rpm on up, with no sign of strain." The *Car and Driver* staff summarized their impressions of the E-Type in their typical, swashbuckling style: "The Jaguar XK-E is one hell of a lot of motorcar-cum-snob-appeal for under $6,000 ($5,858 as tested). Give it another year or two and it'll even make the Queen's list of birthday honors, along with the Rolling Stones."

Road & Track brought the then-current

E-Type's standing against its competition into sharp focus when it tested a Series II coupe along with a Mercedes 280 SL, Porsche 911T, and a Corvette. Looking first at the objective data, *R & T* found that the E-Type was only third fastest overall, with a top speed of 119 mph (remember the E-Type's initial billing as a "150 mph sports car"?), but was quickest in the quarter mile run at 15.7 sec, besting the 300 hp 'Vette by 0.3 sec. The E-Type also won the 0–60 mph contest at 8.0 sec flat, though the Chevrolet had just passed the Jaguar by the 100 mph mark. Porsche's nimble 911 easily won the handling contest at 0.78g on the skid pad; the narrow-tracked E-Type could muster only 0.71g. The Mercedes didn't win any performance category, though the testers acknowledged its comfort and build quality.

Below, printed in England, this factory black-and-white fold-out brochure details all three E-Type models, replete with photos of right-hand-drive models only. None of the cars feature the chromed steel wheels; also shown were the new XJ6 and the 420G, which was still available at the time this folder was printed (April 1970).

Interior revisions are virtually the same as first shown on the 1968 "Series I-1/2" cars, including rocker switches replacing previous toggle units, large clock unit replacing headlight switch, starter button and key lock on center facia, etc. Seats now carry headrests, and all previous brightwork on the dash was now required by federal standards to be finished in non-glare surfaces. Given its budget, Jaguar did an admirable job of meeting the safety requirements while retaining the classic race-inspired interior. *Author photo*

E TYPE OPEN 2 SEATER

ENGINE. Six cylinder 4·2 litre 'XK' engine with twin overhead camshafts and three carburetters. 92·07 mm bore × 106 mm stroke. Capacity 4235 cc, 265 bhp at 5,400 rpm. Compression ratio 9 : 1 (8 : 1 optional.) Cross flow radiator, "No loss" cooling system with thermostatically controlled, electrically driven twin fans.
TRANSMISSION Manually operated four-speed all-synchromesh gearbox. Improved Helix angle for quieter running.
SUSPENSION. (Front) Independent suspension—transverse wishbones and torsion bars and telescopic hydraulic dampers. (Rear) fully independent suspension incorporating, on each side, a lower transverse tubular link pivoted at wheel carrier and subframe adjacent to differential case and, above this, a half-shaft universally jointed at each end. Twin coil springs each enclose a telescopic damper.
BRAKES Servo-assisted disc brakes all round. Independent hydraulic circuits to front and rear brakes.
STEERING. Rack and pinion steering. Collapsible steering column. 2¾ turns lock to lock. Power assisted steering optional extra.
WHEELS AND TYRES. Wire spoke wheels with centre lock hubs. Dunlop SP Sport tyres and tubes. Optional pressed-steel wheels available.
FUEL SUPPLY. 14 Imperial gallon capacity tank. S.U. electric pump.

ELECTRICAL EQUIPMENT AND INSTRUMENTS. Alternator generator. 12-volt battery with negative earth system. Pre-engaged starter motor. Extensive standard equipment includes sealed beam headlamps and headlamp flashing unit, map reading lamp, reversing lamps, flashing direction indicators doubling as hazard warning lights, triple blade two-speed windscreen wipers, windscreen washers, cigar lighter, transistorised clock, automatic ignition advance and comprehensive instrumentation to Jaguar normal high standards.
BODY. Sressed steel two-door two-seater body of monocoque construction. Folding hood with large rear window. (Hard top available as optional extra). Twin semi-reclining bucket seats upholstered in finest quality leather hide over deep Dunlopillo cushions. Deep pile carpets over thick felt underlay.
HEATING AND DEMISTING. High output fresh air heating and multi-point windscreen demisting system. Ducts direct air to each side of car. Two-speed fan.
SPARE WHEEL AND TOOLS. Spare wheel housed beneath boot floor. Comprehensive set of tools. Screw-type easy-lift jack.
PRINCIPAL DIMENSIONS. Wheelbase 8 ft. 0 in., track front and rear 4 ft. 2 in., overall length 14 ft. 7⅞ in., overall width 5 ft. 5¼ in., overall height 4 ft. 0 in., turning circle 37 ft.

E TYPE FIXED

ENGINE. Six cylinder 4·2 litre 'XK' engine with twin camshafts and three carburetters. 92·07 mm bore × 106 mm Capacity 4235 cc, 265 bhp at 5,400 rpm. Compression rat (8 : 1 optional). Cross flow radiator, "No loss" cooling sys thermostatically controlled, electrically driven twin fans.
TRANSMISSION. Manually operated four-speed all-synd gearbox. Improved Helix angle for quieter running.
SUSPENSION. (Front) independent suspension—transver bones and torsion bars and telescopic hydraulic dampers. (R independent suspension incorporating, on each side, a lower tubular link pivoted at wheel carrier and subframe adjacent to d case and, above this, a half-shaft universally jointed at e Twin coil springs each enclose a telescopic damper.
BRAKES. Servo-assisted disc brakes all round. Ind hydraulic circuits to front and rear brakes.
STEERING. Rack and pinion steering. Collapsible steering 2¾ turns lock to lock. Power assisted steering optional extra
WHEELS AND TYRES. Wire spoke wheels with centre lock Dunlop 185 mm × 15 in. SP41HR tyres and tubes. Optional pres wheels available.

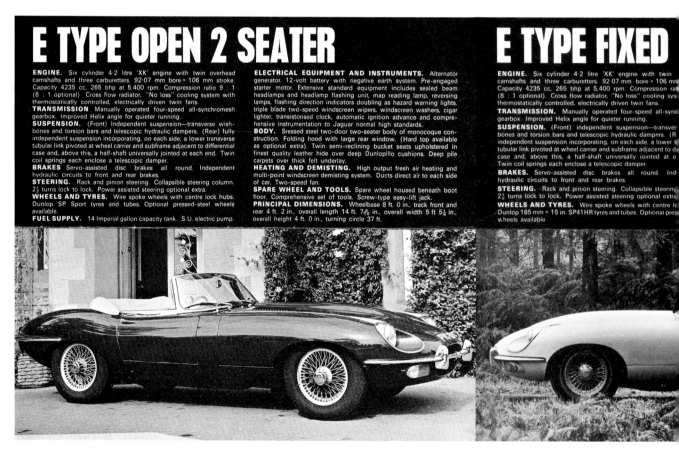

This ad is consistent with the more Americanized designation of the E-Type, the "XKE." Interestingly enough, it also references this model as a "2Plus2." The focus was clear enough; instead of describing the car's race-bred powerplant or fully independent suspension, the copy discusses its optional "power steering, automatic transmission, air conditioning . . ."

Overall, the 911 was *R&T's* top pick on this comparison, though the Jaguar acquitted itself well in several areas. "The Jaguar E-Type's vices and virtues also showed a definite pattern of preference among our drivers. It scored high for ride and overall noise level, but low on ease of entrance, low on seating comfort, low on ventilation and heating and low on outside appearance." Perhaps the exterior changes had taken their toll on the folks at *R & T!*

Road & Track's final comment on this test goes beyond this particular comparison and says much about the E-Type in general: "The word is 'Class.' An undeniable old-world charm . . . the personality would be one that swings. But with dignity."

The last Series II six-cylinder E-Type was produced in September, 1970.

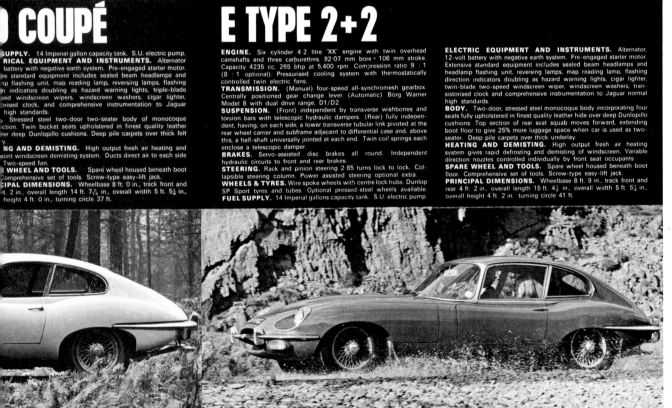

COUPÉ

SUPPLY. 14 Imperial gallon capacity tank. S.U. electric pump.
RICAL EQUIPMENT AND INSTRUMENTS. Alternator, battery with negative earth system. Pre-engaged starter motor. standard equipment includes sealed beam headlamps and ap flashing unit, map reading lamp, reversing lamps, flashing indicators doubling as hazard warning lights, triple-blade ed windscreen wipers, windscreen washers, cigar lighter, rised clock, and comprehensive instrumentation to Jaguar high standards.

Stressed steel two-door two-seater body of monocoque tion. Twin bucket seats upholstered in finest quality leather er deep Dunlopillo cushions. Deep pile carpets over thick felt y.
NG AND DEMISTING. High output fresh air heating and oint windscreen demisting system. Ducts direct air to each side Two-speed fan.
WHEEL AND TOOLS. Spare wheel housed beneath boot omprehensive set of tools. Screw-type easy-lift jack.
CIPAL DIMENSIONS. Wheelbase 8 ft. 0 in., track front and t. 2 in., overall length 14 ft. 7⅜ in., overall width 5 ft. 5¼ in., height 4 ft. 0 in., turning circle 37 ft.

E TYPE 2+2

ENGINE. Six cylinder 4·2 litre 'XK' engine with twin overhead camshafts and three carburetters. 92·07 mm bore × 106 mm stroke. Capacity 4235 cc. 265 bhp at 5,400 rpm. Compression ratio 9 : 1 (8 : 1 optional). Pressurised cooling system with thermostatically controlled twin electric fans.
TRANSMISSION. (Manual) four-speed all-synchromesh gearbox. Centrally positioned gear change lever. (Automatic) Borg Warner Model 8 with dual drive range, D1/D2.
SUSPENSION. (Front) independent by transverse wishbones and torsion bars with telescopic hydraulic dampers. (Rear) fully independent, having, on each side, a lower transverse tubular link pivoted at the rear wheel carrier and subframe adjacent to differential case and, above this, a half-shaft universally jointed at each end. Twin coil springs each enclose a telescopic damper.
BRAKES. Servo-assisted disc brakes all round. Independent hydraulic circuits to front and rear brakes.
STEERING. Rack and pinion steering 2·85 turns lock to lock. Collapsible steering column. Power assisted steering optional extra.
WHEELS & TYRES. Wire spoke wheels with centre lock hubs. Dunlop SP Sport tyres and tubes. Optional pressed-steel wheels available.
FUEL SUPPLY. 14 Imperial gallons capacity tank. S.U. electric pump.

ELECTRIC EQUIPMENT AND INSTRUMENTS. Alternator, 12-volt battery with negative earth system. Pre-engaged starter motor. Extensive standard equipment includes sealed beam headlamps and headlamp flashing unit, reversing lamps, map reading lamp, flashing direction indicators doubling as hazard warning lights, cigar lighter, twin-blade two-speed windscreen wiper, windscreen washers, transistorised clock and comprehensive instrumentation to Jaguar normal high standards.
BODY. Two-door, stressed steel monocoque body incorporating four seats fully upholstered in finest quality leather hide over deep Dunlopillo cushions. Top section of rear seat squab moves forward, extending boot floor to give 25% more luggage space when car is used as two-seater. Deep pile carpets over thick underlay.
HEATING AND DEMISTING. High output fresh air heating system gives rapid defrosting and demisting of windscreen. Variable direction nozzles controlled individually by front seat occupants.
SPARE WHEEL AND TOOLS. Spare wheel housed beneath boot floor. Comprehensive set of tools. Screw-type easy-lift jack.
PRINCIPAL DIMENSIONS. Wheelbase 8 ft. 9 in., track front and rear 4 ft. 2 in., overall length 15 ft. 4¼ in., overall width 5 ft. 5¼ in., overall height 4 ft. 2 in. turning circle 41 ft.

Most Would Rather Fight Than Switch

Swapping an American V-8 engine for a Jaguar XK six (or even a V-12) has been a popular practice for decades. Well, that is, popular among those who perform the work or own such hybrid machines. Jaguar purists shun the very concept. Indeed, many Jaguar clubs will not even allow such a "vile beast" into their concours, nor will said hot rod be considered proper proof of Jaguar ownership for those organizations that require same for membership.

Such swaps occur for a multitude of reasons. One is the search for more power. While we know either Jaguar engine can be modified and built to produce world-beating horsepower, there's little denying that the American V-8s are the least costly way to go fast. You remember the saying: "You can't beat cubic inches." A second factor is that many owners are simply not capable, either in terms of ability or finances, of properly maintaining the multi-carbed, multi-cammed XK. Many who bought E-Types for their unbelievable combination of styling, performance, and value-for-money could ill afford to care for them after they managed to raise the down payment. Cars fell into disrepair, only aggravating their reputation for requiring more-than-average care. Lastly, America is the land of the hot rod, and of the hot rodder, whose credo is "Dare To Be Different."

Are these Yank Tank half-breeds jewels or junk? Treasure or trash? Before we open this Pandora's box, a look at some of the more interesting swap possibilities.

Among the first swap to make big news was *Car and Driver*'s exchanging *not* a Ford or Chevrolet V-8, but a Pontiac OHC six for the tired XK in a 1963 Series I coupe. At first, the swap seemed to make little sense: six cylinders for six, and the new engine rated at nearly 60 hp less than the old. A Muncie four-speed and Hurst shifter were also part of the installation, though they were most likely an improvement over the old Moss box. Performance was almost identical to that of a stock 3.8, though *C&D* noted that the Muncie's tall first gear and the E-Type's 3.31:1 rear end ratio were not an ideal match. Other than gaining an easy-to-care-for powerplant, the results may not have justified the effort. See the July 1966 issue for details.

In 1973, Lockheed engineer Art Harkless didn't want to spend the approximately $800 it would cost to rebuild his 3.8, so he developed a kit to allow the bolt-in installation of a 289/302ci small block Ford into an E-Type. Other Lockheed employees took interest in the swap, and several of them got together to form Logan Engineering. Logan produced and marketed these "XKF V-8" swap kits for several years.

While others have installed Chevrolet V-8s in six-cylinder E-Types, that job requires a bit of torch and hammer work to make the Bowtie engine fit. The Ford, however, is a few inches smaller in most dimensions, requiring no hatchet work (at least with the Logan swap kit) and leaving the owner the option to reconvert to the stock engine, if desired. Either a Ford four-speed manual or C-4 three-speed automatic could be employed; few would argue that American automatic transmissions are among the best in the world. As Carroll Shelby proved, the small block Ford can be easily modified to produce a reliable 300-plus hp, so this swap is definitely one road to a faster E-Type.

Perhaps the king of Jaguar engine swappers is John Radovich, of John's Cars (on Jaguar Lane, of course) in Dallas, Texas. His stock-in-trade is a small block Chevrolet-into-XJ sedan package, but he also markets E-Type conversion products. John's Cars has sold nearly 3,000 V-8 conversion kits and even stocks the hardware to convert the current XJ-40-bodied cars. Its small block Chevy-into-V-12 kit is its most popular E-Type kit, and is sold complete with every nut, bolt, and fitting required to do the job. Also available are Ford V-8-into-six-cylinder E-Type components, but John comments that the Series III conversion is much more popular. John recommends backing the new engine with a GM 700 four-speed overdrive transmission, which, when combined with the E-Type's gearing, gives impressive first gear acceleration yet easy cruising in overdrive.

Radovich comments: "Our conversion is 100 percent bolt-in, including the wiring and A/C. We recommend that people take the stock engine, wrap it in plastic, and set it in the corner of the garage. Twenty years from now, when the fun might have worn off, one can sell the car with both engines, and let the new owner decide whether he wants to keep the car on the road, or put the V-12 back in. The car loses about 150 lb with the conversion, and weight distribution is improved, due to the engine being set further back into the engine compartment. An owner with good mechanical skills and a decent set of tools should be able to do the swap in twenty-five to thirty-five hours, depending upon the amount of detailing they want to do in the engine compartment. When we first started doing conversions, we got a lot of grief from the purists, but a lot of those same people now have a V-8 powered XJ sedan or XJS to drive every day!"

Blasphemy or blessing? You decide.

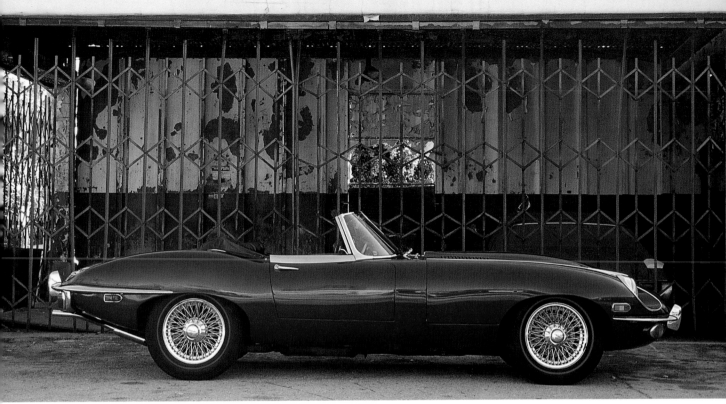

While none of the exterior hardware changes required to meet the new-for-1969 federal U.S. safety requirements could be considered improvements to the E-Type's appearance, the basic shape remained unfettered and undeniably handsome. It's a shame Jaguar stylists could not have integrated the side-marker lights into the front and rear revised bumpers, but dealing with government requirements was a new science in the late-1960s, unlike today, when these features are designed into the car's look from the outset. Cost was also likely a factor at the time. *Author photo*

Front end detail shows heavier chrome bezel for new open headlight design, side-marker light, larger front running light, and heavier front bumper. Though not as stylish as the previously covered headlight, the new open units were easier to maintain and a bit brighter. *Author photo*

Right, series II 4.2 federal-specification engine. The plastic covering usually found around the spark plug wires is not present on this particular car, and the hard-line fuel piping is an aftermarket addition. *Author photo*

89

JAGUAR
6

*There was great pressure to design
the V-12 for Jaguar. Claude Bailey and Bill
Heynes had been working on one, consisting
effectively of two XKs stuck together.
Of course it was a bloody great thing, heavy
and noisy, so Sir William said: 'We'll do
another, one which will be quiet and cheap
to make, and reasonable for its purpose.*
—W.T.F. "Wally" Hassan,
V-12 engine development engineer

1971–1974 Series III 5.3 V-12

There are really at least two parts to the Series III E-Type story: the development of the twelve-cylinder engine that powered it, and the re-engineering that the body/chassis required to make the switch from XK to V-12.

From the perspective of the mid-1960s, a V-12 engine seemed to be one key to future success, both on the race course and in the ranks of exotic street production cars. Ferrari and relative newcomer Lamborghini had each been making their stock-in-trade V-12s for some years. It was well known that Jaguar was looking for more power, and it had seemed that the XK had been expanded about as far as it would go (recall that it was commonly available in 2.4 and 3.4-ltr variants, along with the 4.2). There was also concern about its ability to power larger and heavier cars while continuing to meet increasingly stringent emissions requirements. Jaguar had done testing and development work with Mk X sedans powered by the 4.5-ltr V-8 from the Majestic Major. While these cars easily met the performance criteria, this engine was heavy and also of an older,

A grille fills the E-Type's radiator air intake for the first time; the additional air scoop below is also exclusive to the Series III cars. *David W. Newhardt photo*

This photo was presumably taken at the 1971 New York Auto Show, where the V-12 cars officially premiered in the U.S. It was probably taken shortly after the introductory press conference: note the champagne set up, the vacuum cleaner still on the floor, and the lighting/camera gear laying about. The two women in the car are probably models involved in some publicity photos. *Jaguar Daimler Heritage Trust*

From the rear, the instant telltale sign of a V-12 is the four- (later two-) branch exhaust pipe finisher. This particular car is a 1973 model. *David W. Newhardt photo*

pre-emissions era design, so a Majestic-powered Jaguar never made production.

There was, and is, a lot to be said for V-12 power from a design standpoint. When cast in a 60-degree configuration, and especially when combined with a three-plane crankshaft, a V-12 provides exceptional smoothness. It also allows the combination of larger displacement with a short stroke; a four-cylinder engine tends to be rather rough, and/or requires artificial aids to smooth out secondary imbalances at anything much over 2.5 ltr. This effect is generally reduced

Rear view of partially dressed V-12 engine. Spark plugs are fitted at the top of the head. Even though the engine was designed with pollution controls in mind, a lot of the hardware is still installed externally, and tends to fail with age and heat exposure. Central bellcrank controls four carburetors and is only a bit less complicated to synchronize than the three-carb six-cylinder models. *Jaguar Archives*

as the number of cylinders increases; more power pulses of a smaller size per cylinder make for greater smoothness (the reason that large, twelve-cylinder engines power today's Mercedes Benz, BMW, Ferrari, and, of course, Jaguar flagship models).

V-12 power wasn't totally new to Jaguar; witness the substantial power outputs achieved with the prototype XJ 13's powerplant. This fuel injected, hemispheric-headed racing unit produced well over 500 hp at up to 8,000 rpm, though it was clear that a smaller, lighter, and easily mass-produced design would be required for street use.

Below, carbs aplenty: The four sidedraft Zenith-Stromberg carburetors are tuned to meet emissions requirements of the early 1970s and deliver lower grade fuel than that the previous XKs had to contend with. It is said by some experts that the chrome shields over the top of the engine valley were a late addition, as wet-weather testing revealed water entering the engine compartment via the hood louvers and fouling the electronic ignition componentry. *David W. Newhardt photo*

Series III roadster with its top up is actually a much more pleasant place than were the previous short-wheelbase models, which tended to be a bit claustrophobic. When on the run, there is surprisingly little wind noise and flapping about of the top. Given the quietness of the V-12 engine, normal conversation is possible up to about 80 mph, but because the top is unlined, wind noise does begin to check in above that speed. *David W. Newhardt photo*

This Series III is easily identifiable as a 1973 model; 1971–72 cars carried a rubber-tipped chrome overrider instead of this large chrome one. The 1974 cars suffered with an even larger one! *David W. Newhardt photo*

Right, *Penthouse* magazine's Pet of the Year Cathryn Barrett, who went by the nickname of "Cherokee," was given a 1973 V-12 Roadster as part of the magazine's annual promotion of the "Pet" contest. Besides the magazine promotion, Barrett traveled to the Jaguar factory for photos with company officials and production line workers. *Jaguar Cars Archives*

Bill Heynes and Claude Bailey, who developed the XJ 13 unit, were joined by Walter Hassan and Harry Mundy in heading up the development team for the production V-12. Hassan, who had worked for Jaguar in the past before moving on to Coventry Climax, had been involved with Heynes in the design of the original XK engine. Mundy was another worthy resource gained by Jaguar's purchase of Climax, and the cumulative knowledge possessed by this team of competition-experienced engineers was considerable. Development of the production V-12 unit formally began in 1966.

Front and rear aspect drawings of both Series III models. *Jaguar Daimler Heritage Trust*

Time marches on for both car and makers: Sir William Lyons (right), "Lofty" England, and Series III roadster pose with other great Jaguars of the past at the Jaguar Daimler Heritage Trust museum. *Author collection*

A cast-iron V-12 would have been far too heavy for modern applications, so the designers specified an alloy block with alloy heads, though the block retained iron cylinder liners for more consistent cooling and ease of machining. Although all-alloy engines are quite the norm today, this cost-effective metallurgy was not as well developed at the dawn of the 1970s. A classic example of a failed attempt at using alloy cylinders was Chevrolet's lamentable Vega. Its resultant reputation for oil consumption and engine failures eventually killed the entire line. This would certainly not have been a fate the E-Type deserved.

Logically, the designers chose a 60-degree layout, the bore and stroke measuring 3.54x2.76 in (90x70 mm) for a displacement of 326 ci (5343 cc, or 5.3 ltr). Impressive enough for a large bore sports car, and certainly calculated with installation in the several generation of sedans in mind. The short stroke helped provide for a heady 6,500 rpm redline, 1,000 rpm higher than the smaller XK. Rather than retain the XK and V-12 racing prototype's DOHC design, Jaguar felt that a single overhead cam layout was more than adequate. This was a good call, as the intent was for this engine to be cost-effective to produce in high volume—an extra set of cams, valves, and all the gear required to run them were just extra hardware if Jaguar could attain the desired power output without them. Though cog belts were becoming more and more commonplace on over-head cam engines, Jaguar stuck with chains, as they had this type of system working quite well on the XK by the time the V-12 was on the drawing board. An interesting feature of the alloy head design was that the head was essentially flat. In other words, most of the combustion chamber was actually cast into the piston crown! Mundy and Hassan had experimented with this head design while at Coventry Climax; this and numerous other racing engine design tricks were sure to end up on anything these gentleman worked on. Let's not forget the influence of the ever cost-conscious Sir William: fewer cams, fewer valves, less machining; less money spent.

Fuel injection was employed on the XJ 13 unit and was to be part of the design parameters for the street V-12, but it was ultimately judged too expensive to develop; the only other commercially available system, made by Bosch, was, as used on certain Mercedes models, also quite pricey. In the end, Jaguar stuck with emissions spec Zenith-Stromberg 175 CDSE sidedraft carbs similar in principle to those used on the latest version of the XK, mounted two per head for a total of four. The long intake tracts helped produce a ram effect in the induction tract, increasing low end torque.

While fuel injection fell by the wayside (at least for now), the ignition system was as modern

Optional wire wheel appears quite similar to the Series II's type and retains the same 15-in diameter, but at 6 in it is a full 1 in wider than the previous design. Standard tire size for this larger wheel was an E70/15, approximately equivalent to today's 205/70-15. *David W. Newhardt photo*

The most immediately noticeable change to the interior was the new steering wheel—handsome enough, but lacking in character when compared to the former polished alloy and mahogany piece. Still, it was an inch smaller and, when combined with the now-standard power steering, made for much easier turning, if somewhat at the expense of road feel. The air conditioning unit is also much more integrated into the overall design. *David W. Newhardt photo*

as any available at the time. Jaguar employed an Opus Mark 11 transistorized and breakerless ignition. This system was developed by Lucas for use in Formula 1 racing, so it was more than up to the task in the production V-12. There were no points, and spark timing retained its setting indefinitely. A questionable design decision was the placement of the distributor and transistorized switching module squarely in the middle of the engine valley, in the "V" between the heads. This underhood area retains a considerable amount of heat, and cooked ignition pieces, cracked distributor caps and spark plug wires were commonplace on the earliest V-12s.

Naturally, a full compliment of emissions control hardware was part of the mix, but at least it could be designed as a part of the engine, not just "tacked on" as in the case of the XK. An engine-driven pump injected air into the exhaust port, and a series of valves, hoses, a charcoal canister system, intake retardation controls, and other paraphernalia helped the U.S. and Canadian version of the V-12 meet government specifications. Amazingly, overall weight increase was a scant 80 lb over the iron block XK.

The result? Power and torque ratings significantly exceeding even the pre-emissions era XKs. In U.S. trim, running a 9.0:1 compression ratio, the new V-12 was rated at 314 gross hp at

Right, movie stars and public figures never seemed to be too far away from an E-Type: here, actor Patrick McNee of "The Avengers" poses with a 1974 Series III E-Type at what was most likely one of the series' last new product appearances. *Jaguar Archives*

Behind the Wheel: Series III V-12 Roadster

You know it's going to be different the instant you hear the starter turn. Actually, it still feels strange to light off an old Jaguar without punching a starter button on the dash, but we should have gotten use to that with the end of the Series I E-Types. Anyway, instead of the usual XK "ca-chonk-chonk-chonk" sound, indicating an average number of long strong pistons fighting against compression, you're greeted with a less percussive whirring sound. Did someone leave the spark plugs out? No, it's just the first indication of Jaguar's SOHC V-12.

Even warming up, the engine speaks in velvet tones. Its short stroke and inherently perfect balance send off much less vibration than the six's does. Engage first gear, pull away, and the next big difference surfaces instantly: power steering. Not only do your hands grip a leather wheel, as opposed to the classic, wood-polished alloy piece, but the direct connection to the front wheels experienced in an early E-Type is all but gone. While the new car is wider and heavier, and the power assist is welcome when parking; I miss the road feel of a superbly set up manual rack and pinion. There's little on center action, and just not enough communication. It's no worse than its contemporaries, however, as most manufacturers really didn't learn how to exorcise the "Novocaine" out of most power steering systems until the mid-1980s.

The clutch takes a mighty leg, especially in traffic, but the manual box is a jewel to row through the gears. Throws are short and crisp, and shifting action is still better than that of just about any front wheel drive car out today, some twenty-plus years later.

The immediate question that comes up when comparing the Series III to prior E-Types is "how does the V-12 compare with the six?" Actually, it's not a question of better or worse, the V-12 just very different. The first impression is one of smoothness, from idle to redline; the twelve pulls with a consistent rush of power. The next impression is torque—and lots of it. Gear ratios are well suited to the power band, but it almost wouldn't matter if they weren't, as there is so much torque available that you're only shifting gears because you want to. A short stroke and frequent ignition pulses allow for very low vibration levels. The sound of the exhaust is turbine-like, with a pleasant burble on compression braking, and even a bit more volume would be welcome.

Again begging the comparison to an earlier E-Type, note the acceleration times achieved by *Road & Track* magazine for 1964 and 1972 E-Type coupes:

	6 cyl.	**V-12**
0–30 mph	2.9 sec	3.3 sec
0–60 mph	7.4 sec	7.4 sec
0–80 mph	11.5 sec	12.2 sec
1/4 mile	15.6 sec	15.4 sec

The acceleration times are obviously quite similar; it's just the way the power is delivered that differs so greatly. Even though the Series III had to deal with greater weight and the choking effects of pollution equipment in its design infancy, the V-12 is still a potent automobile by any standard.

The Series III's ride and handling portfolio clearly confirms the car's metamorphosis from "sports car" to "grand tourer." Noticed first is the aforementioned power steering; this is not to say that a sports car can't have it, but it is another subtle indicator of the car's true purpose. The V-12 simply does not feel as nimble nor as attached to the road as an early (say Series I 4.2) E-Type. Its extra weight can be felt, and while the ultimate cornering forces are probably higher than those of an older car, due to the wider track and wider wheel/tire package, the handling is simply not as crisp or communicative.

Comfort is another matter entirely, and this is where the V-12 E outshines its elders. Ride quality is considerably more supple, the longer wheelbase serving up less chop. The revised suspension is considerably more pliant, but not to the point of being mushy—though a tad less body roll would be appreciated. The extra leg room is especially appreciated in the roadster, and especially with the top up. So there, Purists: that 2+2 platform *is* good for something!

The point to be made here is that the experience of driving the V-12 E-Type is more easily compared with that of its early 1970s contemporaries from other marques, and not necessarily with that of six-cylinder E-Types. A lot happened between 1961 and 1974; the driver who enjoys the product of one era might scarcely tolerate that of the other.

6,200 rpm. Max torque was 349 lb-ft at 3,900 rpm. And this was just at the *beginning* of the new engine's development cycle.

But the V-12 is only half of the Series III picture. Jaguar chose to reconcile the E-Type lineup from three models to two, both based upon the longer, 104.7 inch wheelbase of the previous 2+2. The roadster and 2+2 coupe were now the only two body styles available, with the two-place, fixed-head coupe being discontinued. This meant longer doors and more luggage space for the open car and considerable changes beneath the skin on both models.

The front tubular framework required considerable redesign to accommodate the new powerplant; it and the monocoque were strengthened and somewhat stiffened at the same time. The bulkhead was modified to accept a larger bell-housing, and the body panel just below the tail-lights was reshaped to make room for a larger gas tank, now 21.6 gal versus 16.8. A new radiator was employed, while power steering and air conditioning became standard equipment. A General Motors-sourced AC compressor also proved to be a great improvement over the previous unit. The torsion bar front suspension was reconfigured to employ anti-dive geometry, and the front track was widened a substantial 4.5 in. The combination of the wider track and redesigned front sub-frame actually reduced the turning circle over that of the Series II 2+2, from approximately 41 ft to just over 35. The familiar E-Type independent rear suspension was also retained, though rear track was also increased by three inches.

Jaguar's own four-speed manual transmission, introduced on the 4.2 Series I in 1965, was as good as any gearbox available at the time, and fortunately was up to the task of the V-12's torque. It was carried over with virtually no significant changes, save for a larger (10.5 in) clutch. The Borg Warner Model 8 automatic was considered inadequate, however, so a huskier Model 12—still a three-speed unit—was chosen. On U.S. cars, the standard rear end ratio with the four-speed transmission was 3.54:1, while automatic cars got a 3.31:1 rear gear. And for the first time, the automatic transmission was available in the roadster body—yet another subtle indication that the E-Type was heading toward gran touring territory, leaving its elemental sports car roots behind.

Externally, the Series III took on an altogether beefier and more muscular look: the wider track certainly contributed, and the fenders (or "wings," to the British) sprouted wider flares to cover the now 15x6 in wheels. Chrome steel disk wheels with hubcaps became standard fare, while the seventy-two-spoke wire wheels became optional.

For the first time, a grille was found covering the E-Type's radiator opening, and an additional scoop or duct was located just below it. Dual windshield wipers replaced the previous three-bladed design, and out back an all-new muffler arrangement replaced the previous twin "glass pack"-style megaphones. A large, single rear silencer incorporated a unique chrome finisher with four tips (changed to a slightly more conventional twin tip design with the 1973 models).

Stretching the roadster configuration over the longer wheelbase required the design of an all-new removable hardtop. The new top was actually quite handsome and considerably less claustrophobic that those of the earlier, shorter open cars. It also incorporated a vent, or "gill," just aft of the window opening—another attempt to improve the E-Type's less-than-outstanding ventilation characteristics. The roadster's new-found longer wheelbase also made for a handy storage area behind the seats.

Interior modifications were many, with some being improvements and a few being, well, not. The dash was still finished with black, vacu-formed, simulated leather finish. Leather still covered all seats, which were now of the reclining variety, which were mounted on an improved track system with greater fore-aft adjustment.

Much like the late, lamented, dash-mounted starter button, another early E-Type icon was conspicuous by its absence on the Series III: the mahogany and polished alloy 16-in steering wheel. This classic piece gave way to a slightly smaller (15 in) unit, its rim covered in black leather, the spokes now satin-finished aluminum and slightly dished. Though the smaller size was handier, the look was something less than before. The balance of the metal dash pieces, such as the instrument surrounds and heater controls, were also now found in non-reflective finishes. Door pulls and armrests were reconfigured, a safety rearview mirror was added, and a considerable

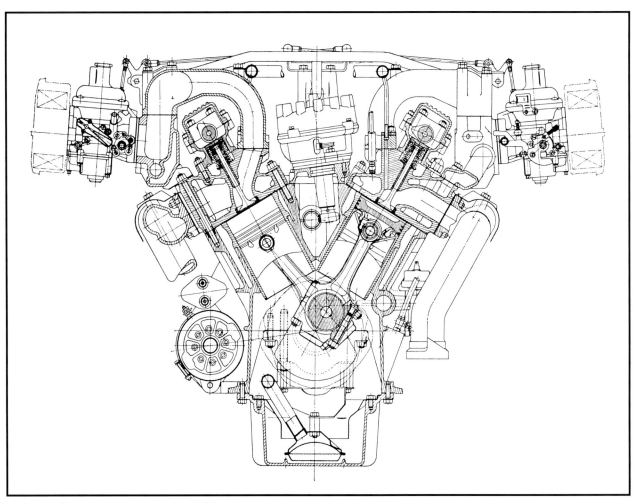

Cross-section drawing reveals architecture of 60-degree V-12. *Jaguar Cars*

amount of sound deadener was placed in the interior, though the previous E-Type could hardly be considered noisy.

It's interesting to note what the sands of time had done to the E-Type's weight and price. In terms of dollars, the car was still considered a bargain, continuing Jaguar's tradition of offering "value for money." A 1972 Porsche 911E Targa listed for just over $9,000; the new-for-'72 Mercedes 350 SL stickered for over $10,500, but an E-Type V-12 roadster ran a mere $7,600. In ten years' time, the E-Type's average price had increased a paltry *$200 per year* on average. The V-12s from Ferrari and Lamborghini were already over $20,000. While the E-Type clearly did well at the cash register, it was not quite so svelte at the scales: while a Series I 3.8 E-Type weighed in at around 2,700lb, a fully equipped Series III roadster with automatic transmission

tipped the scales at a less than sporting 3,500 lb, though a fully equipped Corvette was in the same ballpark.

Smoothness and performance were major goals for the new V-12 engine, and it did not disappoint. *Road & Track* drove an early '71 model and was clearly impressed with the new engine: "The unit does not sound like the exotic Italian V-12s of Ferraris and Lamborghinis. They have a marvelously mechanical sound about them—you're always conscious of the 24 valves working, of camshaft chains, of machinery in general. Exciting sounds. The Jaguar, by contrast, impressed me at first with its extreme refinement. A very quiet idle, and as it was revved up, turbine-like smoothness, if I may use a hackneyed expression." *R & T*'s writer concluded, "the V-12's sound became natural to me, and nothing but its refinement, generous torque and

Factory photo of the V-12 engine as installed in the Series III E-Type. *Jaguar Daimler Heritage Trust*

fascinating exhaust note stuck in my memory after this point."

Nineteen seveny-one and 1972 models were virtually identical, and the E-Type lived out its final two years in relative quiet. There were some changes for 1973 and 1974, and unfortunately few of them were for the good. There was no way to elegantly integrate the 2-1/2 mph front and 5 mph rear bumpers into the E-Type's exposed nose and rounded tail. This late in the car's life, a proper redesign was economically out of the question, so block-like rubber overriders

were added to meet the requirements for 1973. In 1974, the mandate was for 5 mph crash resistance front and rear, so the rubber pieces (on the roadster) just became larger. In Jaguar's defense, many manufacturers came up with solutions that were little better, and some even more ungainly.

For 1973, the compression ratio was reduced more than one full point (from 9.0:1 to 7.8:1), and this reduced horsepower and torque output. Horsepower was now rated at 241 at 5,750 rpm and torque at a still considerable

This page and opposite, the original fixed-head coupe shape had been stretched, widened, and made taller, but it was still unmistakably an E-Type. Serious collectors have not always favored the Series III coupe, but as a reasonably priced classic that's a pleasure to drive and genuinely fast, it's worth a hard look. *David W. Newhardt photo*

Nineteen seventy-one Series III V-12 E-Type 2+2 interior. *David W. Newhardt photo*

Right, all closed V-12 cars are 2+2s and have essentially the same rear seating area as the six-cylinder cars. No V-12 two-place coupe was ever produced by the factory, though a few enterprising shops have built them up: one particularly handsome machine was built from a Series I short-wheelbase roadster but carried a V-12 engine. *David W. Newhardt photo*

285 lb-ft, though care must be taken when making comparisons with any pre-1971 vehicles. Beginning with 1972 models, horsepower quotes were required in SAE net ratings; these take into account an engine running not just alone on a stand, but with certain engine accessories (alternator, power steering pump, etc.) installed as well. A common estimate for the difference between average gross (the old way) and net is approximately 15 percent. Thus, taking the former gross rating of 314 hp and reducing it by 15 percent gives a theoretical net horsepower rating to the higher compression V-12 of approximately 267 hp. So even when equalized for the new rating system, the drop in compression still took a little edge off the V-12 output.

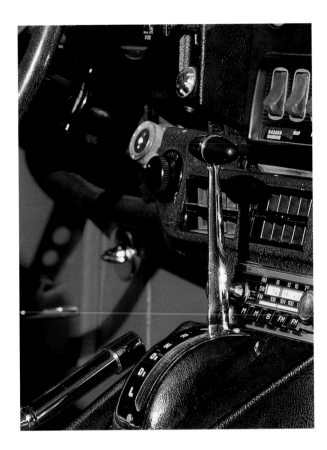

The unique four-branch, chrome exhaust finisher was replaced with a two-outlet design, and seatbelts were slightly revised, as were heater controls. A different steel disk wheel design came on line for the '73 and later cars, using a chrome wheel instead of a painted wheel and chrome trim ring as found on the 1971–72 cars. Heater control markings were changed, and a few other small details were updated to stay in compliance with the ever-changing government regulations, but substantial redevelopment of the E-Type had come to an end by mid-1974.

In early 1974, *Road & Track* published a five-way comparison between the E-Type and its most common competitors in the marketplace: the Chevrolet Corvette, Mercedes 450 SL, Ferrari 246 Dino GTS, and the Porsche 911 Targa. In brief, the E-Type held its own and clearly still excelled in some areas, though its age was beginning to show in a few others: "A drop in compression ratio last year robbed the engine of some of its muscle, and this car couldn't match the straight-line performance of our 1972 test car, but it was still quick enough to tie for second place behind the Corvette in our quarter-mile acceleration trials."

The *R & T* testers gave mixed marks to the Series III's interior packaging, but could not escape recognizing that even while the E-Type was the oldest design in the test, it still had plenty to offer: "Surrounding the magnificent engine is a car that is outdated in several critical areas: seating, interior comfort, controls and ventilation all fall behind the times. But there's still an undeniable old-world charm to the car—wire wheels, impressive looking rocker switches, leather upholstery—that appeals to many. Despite our criticisms, the E-Type is still an exciting car to drive and with the V-12 maintains the Jaguar tradition of offering a lot of car for the money." In short, the test recognized the Mercedes' abilities as a grand tourer (it was only a two-year-old design at the time) and gave the nod to the Ferrari's and the 911's superiority as purer sports cars. The E-Type and Corvette got credit where they always did: performance; heritage; and lots of style for the dollar spent.

It's a natural tendency for enthusiasts, and potential purchasers, to compare the Series III cars with the earlier six-cylinder version; however, there seem to be two distinctly different camps on the subject. There are those who would swear on a stack of shop manuals that the only *pure, real* E-Types are Series I cars. Yet the Series IIIs have shown remarkable popularity among collectors and concours enthusiasts. During the "investment frenzy" of the late 1980s, the highest E-Type prices were being paid for 1974 V-12 roadsters!

Perhaps, if nothing else, it's the undeniable cachet of packing twelve cylinders under that long hood—an attraction still just as valid today.

XJ-13: Misfit or Masterpiece?

Jaguar had little to gain, and an enviable reputation to lose, by a return to Le Mans. C-and D-Types gave Sir William and Company victories in 1951 and 1953 and pulled off a "three-peat" with wins in 1955, 1956, and 1957. Jaguar chose to walk out a winner and pull out of big time racing, just as Mercedes Benz had a few years before. To quote journalist Doug Nye: "In effect, the headline 'Jaguar Beaten' would be hotter news than 'Jaguar Wins.'" Still, only the Indy 500 seemed to have more drawing power for the world's manufacturers than the 24 Hours of Le Mans.

Though the Lightweight E-Types were formidable machines and did have their certain successes, they did not fare well at Sarthe. Nor were they "works" teams in the purest sense. Besides, the Jaguar line-up of the early 1960s was stellar: the still-popular Mk 2; the newly introduced Mark X large sedan; and, of course, the sensational E-Type. Lyons was never one to bite off more than he could chew, but the lure of the French enduro proved simply too attractive; construction of a new works racer began in mid-1965.

While the front-engined, XK-powered C/D-Type's lineage could easily be traced to Jaguar's production models, the XJ-13 was as clean a break from tradition as could be. It was mid-engined, employed an alloy monocoque, and, as a harbinger of things to come, carried V-12 power. However, *this* V-12 was not *that* V-12, the street engine being a completely different beast.

The V-12 destined for the XJ-13 was a purpose-built racing unit, and one need only glance at the specs and power output to be convinced: a 5.0-ltr, 60-degree V-12, all-alloy with double overhead camshafts. Bore and stroke was 87x70 mm. Oiling was via dry-sump, and fuel was dispensed by Lucas mechanical fuel injection. One set of cams was chain-driven, the other gear-driven, and two six-cylinder distributors formed the basis for the Lucas ignition. Early tests of the engine evidenced about 450 hp at 7,000 rpm, and 340 lb-ft of torque. After tuning and development work, the four-cam V-12 was good for more than 500 hp! Backing the engine was a German ZF five-speed transaxle.

The design was another Sayer masterpiece:

Aerodynamicist/stylist Malcom Sayer with a model of the XJ 13 prototype. This model appears to be an early one, as the front hood, air intake, and overall proportion are considerably different than those of the final design. The car in the photo over Sayer's right shoulder is a Lotus Elan. *Jaguar Daimler Heritage Trust*

menacing yet feline, an all-business racer in an elegant tuxedo. Underneath the alloy coachwork was an all-aluminum monocoque, which proved quite stiff in torsional testing. The interior was pure function as well, though the lovely wood and alloy steering wheel reminds you that it's still a Jaguar. The balance of the specifications were typical race car specification for the day: fully independent suspension, huge disc brakes and alloy wheels at each corner, a full compliment of gauges, etc.

In spite of its great promise, the XJ-13 never turned a wheel in competition. There were several complex, and ultimately unfortunate, reasons why.

Race car technology and development were progressing at a torrid pace in the mid-1960s, and several turns of fate seemed to conspire against the XJ-13. After the 1967 running of Le Mans, the CSI (then governing body of international motorsports) announced a maximum engine size of 5.0 ltr for homologated sports cars (fifty or more), and a mere 3.0 ltr for non-homologated or prototype cars. This was no doubt in response to Ford's back-to-back successes at Sarthe with its 427 ci Ford GTs and Mk IVs. There was little chance of Jaguar building fifty XJ-13s to allow use of the 5.0 V-12, so it would have to run in the prototype category. The problem was that Coventry had no 3.0-ltr racing engines, and the Fords could continue to run their 289 V-8s, as more than fifty cars had already been built.

Chief test driver Norman Dewis took the car to MIRA (the Motor Research Industry Association's test facility in Lindly, England) in July of 1967, and though the car was potent in 5.0-ltr form, its road-holding was still not up to snuff with the Ford, Porsche, and Ferrari entries. Richard Atwood and David Hobbs also tested the car, but came to the same conclusion. In short, the already two-year-old race car's competition life was over before it began. The XJ-13 went underground, a fairly well-kept secret, until early 1971.

Jaguar was preparing its launch of the SOHC street V-12 engine, and the Press Office felt it would be smart to strut some heritage by including the twelve-cylinder XJ-13 in some promotional movie footage. Norman Dewis was called upon to pilot the car for the camera, the filming to take place at MIRA, where most of the car's development testing had taken place. With the camera runs complete and the film "in the can," Dewis was completing his final laps when things

The XJ 13 survived its near-fatal crash at MIRA and was beautifully restored by Jaguar and Abbey Panels. It visited America in 1992 as part of Jaguar's support of the Monterey Historic Auto Races at Laguna Seca Raceway. It was also displayed at the Pebble Beach Concours d'Elegance, together with Jaguar's newest mid-engined super exotic, the XJ220. Though the cars were conceived some twenty-five years apart, the similarities are unmistakable. *Author photo*

went awry. Either a rear wheel or a tire came apart, sending Dewis and the XJ-13 into a horrific shunt. It veered up the bank, into the safety fence, and down across the track until it reached the soft, muddy infield. The car flipped, but luckily landed right side up. Norman Dewis was essentially unhurt, though it appeared the car was done for.

Fortunately, not so. Lofty England, who had now assumed the top spot of the retired Sir William Lyons, commissioned a complete restoration of the car in 1972. Fortunately, Abbey Panels retained the body bucks and was able to reconstruct the damaged panels. After a complete—and show quality—restoration, the XJ-13 was shown to the public for the first time in July 1973 at the British Gran Prix. This, some eight years after it was constructed! The car remains the property of Jaguar and is still used at special events, concours, etc., and is often displayed at Browns Lane.

The XJ-13 is a model definition of "too little, too late." It fell victim to the fast pace of racing technology, Jaguar's failure to quickly complete and race it, and some unfortunate rule book changes. As they say, timing is everything.

XJ 13 at MIRA shortly before Norman Dewis' (on right, about to put on helmet) nearly fatal crash. The test probably should have been rescheduled, due to it's just having rained, but as endurance contests are run rain or shine, it is important to gather wet-weather test data. Fortunately, both Dewis and the XJ 13 survived, though the XJ 13's recovery took a bit longer. *Jaguar Daimler Heritage Trust*

A Series III XK?

In spite of the capabilities of the new V-12, and all the hoopla surrounding it, the life of the XK was far from over. It remained the foundation for the new-in-'68, and quite successful, XJ6. Why not a six-cylinder, XK-powered version of the new Series III E-Type chassis?

It was on the drawing board, and was included in early 1971 sales catalogs and Jaguar internal communications. A few were even built: most articles mentioning the six-cylinder Series III estimate that two to three vehicles were produced, though a technical notebook produced by JCNA notes the existence of *six* such cars. Two were labeled as "experimental" machines, though with only half a dozen extant, all of them would have to be considered prototypes. They consisted of both open cars and 2+2s, and though they would certainly not have had the power output of the production V-12 models, they would have to be considered as among the most collectible E-Types ever.

Shown here is the earlier Series III-style steel disk wheel, which featured a chrome trim or "beauty" ring and a simple hubcap. This hubcap design dated back to the 1950s and was used on virtually all other Jaguar models; even the plastic center section could be changed to one inscribed with a "D"—should said cap find its way onto a Daimler, another Jaguar label. Sir William knew how to stretch his money. *David W. Newhardt photo*

As noted, interior ventilation was never an E-Type strong suit, though it was improved on the Series III. This grille, installed on the rear deck lid of the V-12 2+2, relieved air pressure from the interior and further aided flow-through action. *David W. Newhardt photo*

Jaguar V-12: The ultimate cat

Jaguar advertising and sales brochure art played heavily on the feline character of the E-Type, the Jaguar name itself, and the classy but still somewhat sexually charged connection to attractive women: "The Ultimate Cat," "The 12-cylinder Animal," and, certainly one of the catchiest phrases ever employed in Jaguar advertising, "Nobody's Pussycat." *Author collection*

Prowl Car.

Whether cruising on the highway or deftly stalking through twisting country roads, the Jaguar E-type dominates all it surveys. Its styling is so classically distinctive it has been displayed at the Museum of Modern Art.

Beneath that sculptured surface lurks engineering that traces its breeding to the legendary Jaguar victories at the 24-Hour Race of Le Mans.

Jaguar's independent suspension front and rear lets the graceful cat keep all four feet on the ground, silky even on rough terrain.

The four wheel disc brakes are ventilated in front and mounted in-board in the rear. All E-types are complete with Dunlop Sport 70 whitewall belted radials.

The incredible Jaguar V-12 aluminum alloy engine gives the word "smoothness" a new standard to live by. Its 326 cubic inches of capacity is considerably smaller than the 468 cubic inches of capacity of the average American luxury V-8.

In addition to the luxury, comfort and instrumentation that you expect in a Jaguar, there is that indefinable quality in the Jaguar E-type that gave this automobile its name. Jaguar, a magnificent beast, wild of spirit but in full control of its powers, exuberant yet disciplined.

See it now at your Jaguar dealer. For his name and for information about overseas delivery, call (800) 447-4700. In Illinois, call (800) 322-4400. Toll Free.

BRITISH LEYLAND MOTORS INC., LEONIA, N. J. 07605

Jaguar

Nobody's Pussycat.

Of all the sports cars available to you, this is the one—the ultimate cat.

Because it offers what the others can't offer: the Jaguar V-12 engine.

And that changes the discussion from *what* a sports car can do to *how well* it can do it.

That's what the Jaguar E-type V-12 is all about. How well it glides from zero to fifty. How well it accelerates out of a pack and into the clear. Even how well it behaves in downtown traffic at quitting time before a holiday weekend.

In a word, the Jaguar V-12 is smooth. It's smooth going up the scale from zero and it's smooth going from cruising speed to passing speed. It's even smooth waiting for the light to change.

Because, from an engineering viewpoint, the Jaguar V-12 is in perfect balance. Since its 5.3 litres of capacity are divided by twelve—not eight or six—the forces are spread more evenly over the crankshaft by delivering smaller but more frequent pulses of power.

What is the effect like? Well, it's something like a turbine. And it's something like an express elevator. But it's not *exactly* like anything else. That's why you have to drive a Jaguar E-type V-12 before you decide on anybody else's sports car.

Since it is a Jaguar, it has independent front and rear suspension with "anti-dive" control. Power-assisted rack and pinion steering. Power-assisted disc brakes on all four wheels—ventilated in the front. A four-speed manual is standard, an automatic is optional.

So see the Jaguar E-type V-12. It's the only production V-12 sports car in town. And that makes it second to none.

For your dealer's name and for information about overseas delivery, call (800) 447-4700. In Illinois, call (800) 322-4400. Calls are toll free.

BRITISH LEYLAND MOTORS INC., LEONIA, N. J. 07605

Jaguar

JAGUAR 7

This is the last car built after thirteen years' manufacture of the Jaguar 'E' Type Sports Cars. Sir William Lyons, President, Jaguar Cars Coventry, 1974.
—text of a small metal plaque affixed to the dashboard of Series III E-Type roadster, chassis number IS 2872

Fade to Black: The Last Fifty E-Types and the XJS

It's difficult to pinpoint a single reason for the E-Type's demise, if for no other reason than that there were so many reasons, so much timing at play.

Recalling the climate of the early 1970s, the automobile was a none-too-popular element of society. The world, particularly the United States, was experiencing its first postwar "Gas Crunch." Whether real or contrived (yet another worthy book subject), the oil embargo wrought literal panic in the streets, and lines at the gas pumps. Gas prices doubled in short order, and mandatory rationing nearly became a reality. Fuel mileage became the number one factor to consider when purchasing an automobile: "MPG" replaced "0–60" in manufacturers' advertisements practically overnight. In the midst of this reactionary mind-set sat the still splendid, though somewhat thirsty E-Type, replete with its V-12 engine and *four* carburetors! To put it succinctly: wrong car, wrong time.

End of the line: Chassis IS 2782 makes its way down the temporary assembly line. The final E-Types were produced in a smaller facility away from the main plant, which had to be retooled to accommodated XJ6 production. Could there be a more valuable E-Type? *Jaguar Daimler Heritage Trust*

Group 44 Gets an "E" Ticket Ride
by Patrick C. Paternie

Le Mans may be as integral to Jaguar racing lore as British Racing Green, but Summit Point, West Virginia, was where Jaguar really began writing one of the most successful chapters in its competition history.

Group 44, an organization founded by Bob Tullius and the late Brian Fuerstenau, used Summit Point as a test track for the MGs and Triumphs with which they dominated their classes in SCCA road racing during the 1960s and early 1970s. The team was closely linked to British Leyland. When Jaguar became part of the fold, Tullius began to push for a 4.2 XK-E to race, later eyeing the V-12 version when it debuted.

"We always wanted to move up to a class where we could win the feature race of the day," recalls Tullius, in reference to the A- and B-Production race groups where Corvettes and Cobras ruled the roost.

Tullius got his wish in 1974, when Michael Dale, then vice president of sales for Jaguar and faced with a glut of V-12 E-Types cluttering the docks in this country, agreed that the best way to sell them was to go racing. The Jaguar fac-

Another victory wave from Bob Tullius at the wheel of the Group 44 Jaguar E-Type V-12. *Jaguar Archives*

tory, despite its history and racing tradition, did not have the means at the time to mount a racing effort. That assignment was split between two teams in the U.S.—Joe Huffaker on the West Coast and Group 44 on the east coast.

Not only was Jaguar hedging its bet, and its reputation, by utilizing two teams, it was, according to Tullius, waiting until those teams proved they could win before issuing press releases sanctioning the effort. Officially, the program was part of the U.S. sales organization.

Working under tight SCCA-imposed restrictions, Fuerstenau and Tullius took a production car and strengthened the rear suspension to handle the increased loads imposed by racing. This process included mounting a set of the larger, ventilated front brakes to the rear as well. An even bigger challenge facing the team was the oiling system of the V-12 engine. The SCCA would not approve a dry-sump, so Fuerstenau toiled long and hard to develop an oil pan that would prevent sloshing and provide adequate oil pickup. When all was said and done, Tullius estimated the V-12 was capable of putting out about 450 horsepower, very close to what Huffaker had developed. Both cars made their racing debut over the weekend of August 10–11, 1974.

One notable example of cooperation between the teams did occur that weekend. Tullius had broken the B-Production lap record and was leading at Watkins Glen with three laps to go when the gearshift lever broke! Huffaker, on the West Coast, was racing at Seattle International later that weekend. As a preventative measure, a phone call was made to Huffaker, informing him of Group 44's shifter problem. Huffaker's driver, Lee Mueller, encountered no such difficulties en route to a new lap record, and easily won the race.

The next weekend, fittingly at Summit Point, Group 44 notched its first victory. From then on, Tullius raced and won at Gainesville, Bryar, Nelson Ledges, and Bridgehampton. He was the 1974 B-Production Champion for SCCA's North Eastern Region, earning him a trip to Road Atlanta for the National Championship Runoffs. Mueller, in Huffaker's Jaguar, also reached the Runoffs as Northern Pacific champ.

At Road Atlanta, Tullius qualified on the pole, with Mueller next to him on the grid. Things went downhill for Jaguar from there. The Huffaker car suffered a flat tire in the early laps while Tullius forged a lead. As the race wore on, however, Tullius' tires wore down to the point that a Corvette was able to catch and pass him on the last lap. Group 44's Jaguar did hang on to finish second.

The reason for the Jaguar's tire problems can be traced to the SCCA rules, which allowed wheels to be 1.5 in wider than stock. Corvettes came with 8.5-in wheels, allowing them to race on 10-in rims. The XK-E was fitted with a 6.5-in wheel as standard, thus limiting it to 8-in race wheels. Additionally, the car suffered from a narrow track in relation to its overall length.

Nineteen seventy-five saw Group 44 solve its tire problem and go on to win six times—five for Tullius and one for Fuerstenau in the last race of the season. Tullius had amassed enough points to qualify for the Runoffs, so Brian, who usually raced an MGB, was given the reins of the Jaguar.

Another interesting footnote to the 1975 season was that the V-12 and the team's Triumph TR-6 were both entered in a Trans-Am race at Brainerd. The Jag was running in the top three when it broke a rear axle and retired. Tullius remembers the TR-6 going on to finish in third place.

At the 1975 Runoffs, all the drama took place on the pace lap—actually, pace laps. The race proved to be anticlimactic, with the Group 44 Jaguar winning easily.

Tullius recalls that the Jaguars had qualified one-two: "In the warmup, Sunday morning, Lee was coming down the back straight and heard this terrible noise, so he shut it down and came into the pits saying that the gearbox was broke.

continued on next page

Huffaker's guys frantically changed the gearbox. They did not check the gearbox but took Mueller's word for it. The car sat there the rest of the day until it was time for the race and then they pushed it to the false grid.

"We all got in the cars and headed onto the track behind the pace car. About three corners later, looking out of the corner of my eye, I don't see Mueller. He disappeared. I thought he'd catch up in a little bit. As we came up under the bridge I determined that he was not there and I didn't want to start the race without him. I accelerated away from the pack so that the starter couldn't possibly give us a green flag. I was twenty-five to thirty car lengths ahead of the second place car to purposely break the start and make us do one more pace lap. I wanted to give him [Mueller] a chance to catch up.

"Then we got to the corner where I first saw him disappear. His car was on a tow truck as they were taking it back to the pits. The rest of the story is that they got it back and discovered that the transmission was not broke but there had been a failure in the rear end. Mueller's analysis of what was wrong was incorrect. They had changed the wrong component and the original problem manifested itself again on the third turn just as it had on the straight in the morning's warmup."

Huffaker and Group 44 faced off one more time in an exhibition race at Laguna Seca in late 1976, when Jaguar was the featured marque of the Monterey Historic Races. This time, it was Tullius who suffered a tire puncture on the final lap.

That was the last time the V-12 was raced by Group 44. The car was scheduled to be retired at the end of 1975, the street version already out of production, but teething problems with their XJ-S forced the team, early in 1976, to run the car in three events to earn championship points.

Group 44 is no longer in the race car business. It still exists, providing vintage car restoration services. After competing in the Trans-Am series in 1990 for Pontiac, Tullius turned over the shop to his crew chief, Lanky Foushee. Tullius currently focuses his energies on a collection of World War II aircraft, being an avid history fan of this era. Still, he holds fond memories of the E-Type: "You always like cars you win with, and I won a lot with it. That engine was probably the most durable production engine ever built. We *never* lost an engine. I enjoyed racing such a prestigious name. There was a nostalgia to racing a Jaguar—becoming part of that history was enjoyable. Finally achieving a goal of winning main events—that endears it to me a great deal."

Appropriately enough, the all-conquering Group 44 Jaguar V-12 is now owned by Jaguar Cars and resides at Browns Lane.

Remember, too, that manufacturers were caught up in the need to deliver cars meeting tougher and tougher emissions and safety requirements. Jaguar had managed to refit the old XK engine to meet emissions specs, and the V-12 was designed with that in mind as well, but 1975 would bring about even tougher requirements, such as catalytic converters, an item not likely to package well in the E-Type's exhaust system. The car's looks were also suffering further indignities, given the new bumper requirements imposed in 1973; the rubber protuberances grew even more ungainly on the 1974 models. There was also considerable fear at the time that convertibles and roadsters would be banned altogether in the U.S.

market, and the V-12 Roadster made up more than 50 percent of the E-Type's sales.

The combined effect of the above essentially put high-profile, high-performance automobiles out of step with the era. The E-Type was far from the only casualty: the DeTomaso Pantera, another high-performance car of exceptional value, went by the wayside, as did the Ferrari Daytona. Ferrari had no intention of bringing its replacement, the Berlinetta Boxer, to the U.S. market. The Ford Mustang became little more than a chrome-plated Pinto for the 1974 model year. There was even speculation among the automotive press that the Corvette might be on its last legs.

Though it's a simple matter to point fingers

Team photo of the crew that assembled the last E-Type. Is it possible some of the older chaps may have been around to assemble the first ones? *Jaguar Daimler Heritage Trust*

This is the last car built after thirteen years' manufacture of the Jaguar 'E' Type Sports Cars.

W. Lyons

Chassis No. IS 2872

Sir William Lyons. President. Jaguar Cars. Coventry. 1974.

Dash plaque affixed to Chassis IS 2872. Enough said. *Jaguar Daimler Heritage Trust*

at external factors contributing to the E-Type's demise, there is one other less tangible but no less significant element: *it was time.* Jaguar's model cycles tend to run on the long side, but ten years was about average. The E-Type had gone better than that by 30 percent, and was beginning to show its age a bit. The XJS was already under development, and was intended to be V-12-powered from the beginning, but the new car would certainly not be ready for production by 1971, so the E-Type was reconfigured to house the new engine. It would not have been right to simply continue hanging on more and more hardware in an effort to keep an aging,

115

The final E-Type, finished in black and never sold by the factory, is now held in the Jaguar Daimler Heritage Trust Collection at Browns Lane. *Jaguar Daimler Heritage Trust*

though undeniably classic, design up-to-date with requirements that couldn't even have been imagined at its genesis. The E-Type deserved better.

Recall that there was at least some genuine concern that the convertible would be legislated out of production. Irrespective of lawmakers, the market itself seemed to be turning its back on the ragtop: several nameplates previously available in convertible or roadster form were not continuing with an open platform at new model time. Examples: the 1974 Ford Mustang; 1970 Camaro/Firebird; 1976 Corvette; Ferrari Boxer (replacing the Daytona); Maserati Khamsin (replacing the Ghibli); and the new "SLC" model that Mercedes had added to the previously roadster-only SL line. It's no surprise, then, that Jaguar's new-for-1975 XJS

was available as a closed coupe only.

Other indications that Jaguar intended to flavor the XJS as more of a luxury GT than a pure sports car were evidenced by some of the equipment listed as standard on the S that were either optional, or not even *available*, on early E-Types: automatic transmission (no four-speeds for U.S.-specification cars); air conditioning; power steering; etc. In typical Jaguar fashion, even though the company was Leyland-owned and Sir William Lyons had retired some three years prior the XJS's 1975 introduction, a considerable bit of the new car's hardware was carried over from the last E-Types. The V-12 engine and Borg Warner automatic transmission, of course, along with the amaz-

E-Type and V-12 Archives: Jaguars on Tape

Many books contain a bibliography, or at least an "Additional Reading" list of other titles the reader may wish to consult. This one is no exception, and it suggests several worthwhile efforts. Still, with the proliferation of home video, many enthusiasts are building automotive tape libraries to rival their book collections.

There are several tapes on the market that are devoted to Jaguars, or that at least cover Jaguars to some extent, but the first two that any Browns Lane worshiper should acquire are *The Jaguar E-type Archive* and the *Jaguar V12 Archive*. Both are produced by Porter Publishing Ltd./PP Video Productions in England, and both are basically collections of factory footage, promotional spots, and documentary short films.

Naturally, the *E-type Archive* will be of the most interest to readers of this book. The tape opens with snippets of Jaguars at shows, on track, and with some factory promotional shots, giving a taste of what is to follow. The first segment, and perhaps the best of them all, is priceless footage of the E1A prototype being tested at MIRA, the British Motor Industry Research facility. At the wheel (of course) is perennial Jaguar test pilot Norman Dewis. E1A is shown on the banked turns, then on the skid pad. It is here we see first hand how badly the "Blind Mole" prototype oversteered—there was much work yet to be done. There are even a few moments of recently discovered *color* footage, a rare and worthwhile find.

Next up is some promotional tape with not-yet-Gran Prix champion John Surtees visiting the factory to collect one of the first roadsters. This is raw tape, and shows several different angles of the same scene.

Whatever your feeling about the 2+2, few would enjoy seeing one deliberately destroyed, as in the footage covering government crash testing. The slow-motion film demonstrates the E-Type's structural integrity, as the car appears quite intact from the windshield rearward.

A rather long segment illustrates a U.S. owner collecting his car from a Jaguar agent in Paris, then touring Europe with it before shipping it home to New York. While beautifully photographed, it gets a little tiring, even though the scenery is spectacular. Restorers will cringe at the sight of a large, roof-mounted luggage rack being screwed into place!

The final segment is a documentary short film covering Group 44's 1975 SCCA championship. Bob Tullius and his immaculate V-12 roadster were clearly the crowd favorites, and were equally the measure of the largely Corvette-dominated field. The sounds are magnificent, and the footage provides a fitting denouement to the E-Type's racing career in the U.S.

The *V12 Archive* focuses more on the engine: it is seen in E-Types, and XJS models, and even the most recent XJ12 promotional tape is included. The coverage of Tullius and the Group 44 is expanded to several segments, but the pearl here is a long and detailed interview with the V-12's creators, Walter Hassan and Harry Mundy. A mockup engine revolves on a stand in front of the men, and hearing them describe the development and engineering of their pet project is great fun. We also see the XJ 13 prototype performing for the camera just prior to its horrific crash, and there is some choice footage of the V-12 launch promotional at Warwick Castle.

Both tapes are a worthwhile addition to any E-Type fan's collection. The were produced in 1993, and are available (as of this writing) from PP Video Productions, The Storehouse, Little Hereford Street, Bromyard, Herefordshire, HR7 4DE, England (Telephone 0885-488800). They have also appeared in the EWA (Eric Waiter and Associates) Catalog. As they are produced in Europe, remember to specify "VHS" format (as opposed to the European "PAL" format) if you intend to watch on a U.S.-specification VCR.

The XJS was a clean break from the E-Type, a clear step toward a luxury grand tourer, and a decided move away from the E-Type's first role as a sports car. Jaguar's mis- sion with the XJS was clear: it was available as a coupe only, and in the U.S. employed only the V-12 engine and an automatic transmission. *Author collection*

ingly little-changed independent rear suspen-sion—even then a nearly twenty-five-year-old design. Still, it would not have been proper to call the XJS anything but a virtually new car, as the chassis, coachwork, and interior were obvi-ously a complete break from the E-Type's.

Not long ago, England's *Performance Car* magazine performed an interesting "Then and Now" sort of comparison, pitting a 1965 4.2 Coupe against a 1991 XJS. Both were painted red, and both carried six-cylinder engines with manual gearboxes. The editors were astute enough to make allowances for this particular E-Type's 96,000 miles. Their findings confirmed the two machines' divergent philosophies and personalities: "In the way they sit to the road, there's a full 30 years between them. The broad-shouldered XJS's arches are full of wheel and tyre and it seems to hug the ground. The E-Type is no less aggressive but its slim wheels and

tyres are tucked into the shadows beneath the body . . . It's hard to believe that the same man, Malcom Sayer, styled both."

The sports car versus GT aspect was well summarized by editor John Barker, who noted that "although the XJS is the finer handling car here, the E-Type is the natural sports car. The 4-litre Sports Pack XJS might be the closest we've come to an E-Type replacement, but its forte remains its ability to cover long distances in supreme com-fort." Newer, yes; better in many ways, perhaps; but a different breed of a different era, to be sure.

Interestingly enough, production of the 2+2 E-Type wound down first. A strange quirk in the new safety laws, one of many, involved rollover protection standards for closed cars that were *not* applicable to open machines! Reverse discrimination? Perhaps.

In laudatory, though somewhat funereal acknowledgment, the last fifty E-Type roadsters, save the penultimate, were painted Sable Black (the odd duck was finished in British Racing Green). Each was affixed with a metal dash plaque acknowledging its membership in this somewhat somber, though now highly prized, group of E-Types. Fortunately, Jaguar documented the occasion well, taking many photographs of the final cars as they were built on their temporary assembly line, as well as of the workers who assembled them. The main assembly area had already been cleared for XJ6/12 production.

The XJS replaced the E-Type chronologically, and also in Jaguar's line-up, but not in purpose or in character. Jaguar had segued from a sports car that had aged but grown fairly well into a GT, to a clearly purpose-built grand touring coupe. Even at the time, road testers and enthusiasts alike mourned the E-Type's passing, and greeted the uniquely styled XJS with an occasionally tepid welcome. It's interesting to note that the XJS has ultimately outlived and outsold the E-Type: as of this writing, the XJS is entering its twenty-first year of production, though its appeal has been greatly expanded, with both six- and twelve-cylinder versions available in both coupe and convertible form. Sales have topped

Though the XJS never did cause the stir that the E-Type did, it ultimately lived a longer production life and yielded greater sales numbers for Jaguar. Six-cylinder versions came along in the late-1980s, and a factory-produced convertible soon followed. This 1995 4.0 Convertible carries the latest AJ16 six-cylinder engine and represents the XJS's twenty-first year in production. *Jaguar Photo*

100,000 units. The V-12 engine itself is a much-developed descendant of the one introduced in the Series III E-Type, though it is now a fully modern, computer-controlled, fuel injected wonder, producing better than 300 horsepower. One hopes that it, too, will enjoy a forty-year production life, like the XK six before it.

The final Jaguar E-Type, chassis #2872, carrying engine #7S17201SA, was produced in September 1974, is owned by Jaguar Cars, and resides at Browns Lane.

The E-Type's day was done, but certainly not the V-12 engine's. Bob Tullius continued his relationship with Jaguar, and together they re-entered international sports car and endurance competition. Though Tullius was not successful at winning Le Mans for Jaguar (that particular spoil went to the Tom Walkinshaw Racing teams in both 1988 and 1990), the always-immaculate Group 44 XJRs did notch their fair share of wins in IMSA competition. This XJR was photographed at the Los Angeles Times 6-Hour enduro at the now-defunct Riverside International Raceway. *Author photo*

F(-Type) + F(ord) = DB7

Jaguar, like any manufacturer, works continuously to refine, update, and upgrade its products. Part of the process is developing a series of design studies and prototypes. Some clearly lead to future models; many end up out in the back lot, crushed, or never even make it out of the design phase.

E-Types of this sort fall basically into two categories: projects undertaken while the E-Type was in series production, and cars that may have been intended as descendants. While many people (including me) would argue that the E-Type can never be replaced, there have been hints over the years that another sports car—an F-Type, if you will—would emerge from the Jaguar line-up. As of this writing, it hasn't happened yet, but the possibility appeared closer than ever in the fall of 1989.

At that time, car magazines, especially British ones, erupted with spy photos of a new

F-Type. *Car* magazine featured the car on its October 1989 cover, reporting:

Jaguar will re-enter the sports car market in 1993, after an absence of almost 20 years, when it launches this car, the F-type. Designed to replace the E-type, production of which ceased in 1975, the new F-type will be available both as a roadster and a coupe.

Power comes from a choice of two engines: a 4.0-litre straight-six unit (as used in the new 4.0-litre XJ6), and a twin turbo version of the same motor, which may produce as much as 400 BHP. Another interesting feature of this F-Type would have been the prospect of four-wheel drive, a Jaguar first. The system was to be developed with FF Developments, who had done the four-wheel drive hardware for the Jensen FF, among other British cars.

The project was dubbed the "XJ-41," as it was based upon redone XJ-40 componentry;

Cousins Beneath the Skin: E-Type and stillborn XJ-41 "F-Type" styling cues are clearly visible in the new Aston Martin DB7. The DB7 also uses an engine architecturally similar to the supercharged AJ16 used in the 1995 Jaguar XJR sedan. *Photo courtesy of Aston Martin Lagonda*

development work began in 1986, just as the new XJ6 was coming to market. It was also to employ XJ6 suspension—sort of an odd reverse twist of fate, as the original XJ6 used E-Type-based suspension! Germany's Karmann coach-works reportedly built the prototypes; the roadster would have most likely been a pure two-seater, while the coupe, in E-Type vernacular, would have been more correctly called a "2+2." Styling was done by Jaguar's in-house styling department.

Nineteen ninety-three came and went: no F-Type. What happened? While the details of this particular prototype's demise would probably fill a book of their own, two major factors stand out. The short story is that, when Ford bought Jaguar, it reorganized the British company's priorities; the F-Type, as it was, did not fit the mix. Ford correctly assessed that the XJS, already more than ten years old at the time, would need a redo, and that the XJ6 would also have do be worked over to compete with an ever-increasing (and improving) market full of luxury sedans. Even with Ford's backing, only so much could be done at once.

Furthermore, with all the weight and cost added by things like four-wheel drive and twin turbos, it was questioned whether the car was really an appropriate E-Type replacement, anyway. To quote Michael Dale, president of Jaguar Cars, Inc., U.S.A.: "Ultimately, we ended up with too small an engine in too heavy a car, and it wasn't a sports car any longer." At least, it wasn't a Jaguar any longer.

Though both companies officially deny that the F-Type prototype ultimately became the Aston Martin DB7, the ancestral connection is undeniable, right down to the use of a super-charged, twin cam six; the F-Type was also rumored to be considered for an Eaton super-charger as an alternative to the twin turbos. The size and dimensions are about right, and don't forget the umbilical connection via Ford.

It now appears that the best bet for a spiritual successor to the E-Type will be embodied in the upcoming replacement for the XJS. Look for it as a 1997 model.

Out in a blaze of glory (or at least in a blaze of tire smoke), the V-12 E-Type attained some of the line's most notable race victories after E-Type production had officially ended. At left is the Group 44, SCCA championship E-Type driven by Bob Tullius; on the right is Lee Mueller piloting the Huffacker Engineering V-12. The cars here were photographed competing in a match race at Laguna Seca Raceway in 1976. *Lance Iverson Photo, courtesy of Jaguar Archives*

A 1971 Series II? It may have been possible, at least according to this factory postcard, which outlined a "1971 XKE Convertible" in full Series II trim. This is not to be confused with the longer-wheelbased V-12 Series III roadster, or the prototype Series III cars carrying six-cylinder engines. Of course, the postcard also says: "Specifications subject to change without notice." Change they obviously did . . . most likely at the last minute. *Author collection*

Interview with Michael Dale, president, Jaguar Cars, Inc., USA August 1994

Author: From your perspective, after thirty-five-plus years of involvement with Jaguars, what overall impact would you say the E-Type had upon Jaguar as a marque?

Dale: I think the E-Type became the soul of Jaguar, particularly in North America. It's the car that when you're sitting on an airplane and someone finds out you work for Jaguar, they always say to you 'when are you going to make another E-Type?' It was far bigger than its sales or its commercial success. People fell in love with the car. I think it [the Jaguar mystique] really had been building from the [XK] 120 through the 140 and 150, but the E-Type was the car that set everybody on fire.

Author: Why did the new Aston Martin DB7 get built, and not an E-Type replacement/F-Type?

Dale: A lot of the things that were going to be done around [the XJ] 41 [platform] had to be dropped because we started off working on a different platform. Anything we do in the sports area in the future is going to come off the S platform. 41 in theory started off with the 40; it was carved up and changed. It was widened because we wanted to make it four-wheel drive, and it became heavier with more metal in it. Ultimately we ended up with too small an engine in too heavy a car, and it wasn't a sports car any longer.

Author: In other words, it wouldn't have been an E-Type?

Dale: Oh no. In its original concept at the styling stage, it would have been. We tried to do too much with it. It's very difficult to take a platform off a sedan and make it into a sports car. We failed.

Author: I appreciate your candor. Although the XJS chronologically followed the E-Type, it was never intended as a direct philosophical replacement. To what do you attribute the S-Type's ultimately outliving—and outselling—the already legendary E-Type?

Dale: Because an E-Type, while extremely beautiful and a very exciting vehicle, was not a very practical car. It wasn't an easy car to live in. You switch the air conditioning on and you could see the temperature gauge rise. It just wasn't a practical form of transportation. An XJS is.

Author: We've seen mockups of cars and prototypes that have a lot of E-Type cues in them. Is this a new S-Type or E-Type?

Dale: It's a more sporting vehicle. I always have trouble trying to say if [the future vehicle] is a new S-Type or an E-Type. It combines the best features of both of them, which is going to mean it will hit the market right dead center. A very beautiful package.

Author: Will it replace the current S-Type, or be built alongside it?

Dale: It will [replace it] on the production line, yes. Whether it will replace it in people's minds, we shall have to see. Nobody's ever asked me when we were going to make another XJS.

Author: But they do ask when you're going to make another E-Type?

Dale: That's right.

Author: Is this car more S-Type or E-Type?

Dale: I think it will be halfway between the two, but I think that the popular myth will be that it's a real replacement for the E-Type. People will see that, in terms of its soul as it were, the XJS, while it's a lovely car, and wins beauty contests all over the place, has never become the soul of Jaguar. I think the new car will . . .

Epilogue

The E-Type survives today as one of the most instantly recognized automobiles on earth, a landmark of automotive beauty and design, and one of the most prized collectibles of the 1960s and early 1970s. Fortunately, an immensely strong international enthusiast club network ensures the car's immortality. Equally important is the huge aftermarket support available. There are dozens of companies reproducing parts for the E-Type, and there are countless restoration and repair shops that cater to E-Types as a specialty. It is possible, though not always cost-effective, to restore an E-Type from practically any condition to concours-winning standards.

Is it, or was it ever, the perfect car? Hardly. The E-Type's occasionally spotty electrics and cooling and sometimes marginal-quality control would keep it off any such list. However, today's restoration techniques and aftermarket parts can allow an E-Type owner to upgrade his machine substantially without significantly compromising its originality. The car also continues to make a lot of lists: "Ten Greatest" lists; "Most Beautiful Cars of All Time" lists; "Good Investment" lists; and, most importantly, classic car buyer's *Wish Lists.*

There are other cars that are faster, smoother, rarer, more comfortable, more reliable, possess a greater racing history, or are able to best the E-Type in one or a few of many other categories. But there are few cars that have engraved themselves so indelibly on the hearts of automotive enthusiasts the world over. Its time as a production automobile has truly come and gone, but its future as an all-time great sports car is absolutely assured.

Appendices

Specifications

Series I 3.8 Roadster

Number of Units Produced	7,827

Dimensions

Overall Length (inches):	175.0
Wheelbase (inches):	96.0
Width (inches):	65.2
Height (inches):	48.1
Track (inches):	50.0
Curb Weight (pounds):	2,770.0

Engine

Number of Cylinders:	6
Layout:	Inline; DOHC
Construction:	Alloy head; iron block
Bore x Stroke (inches):	3.43x4.17
Displacement (cc/inches):	3781/230.6
Compression Ratio:	9.0:1
Horsepower Rating @ rpm	265 @ 5500
Torque Rating @ rpm (lb-ft):	260 @ 4000
Intake/Carburetion:	three SU sidedraft

Drivetrain

Standard Transmission:	Four-speed manual (non-synchro first)
Optional Transmission:	N/A
Standard Differential Ratio:	3.31:1

Chassis and Suspension

Frame Type:	Monocoque w/front subframe
Brake Type:	Four-wheel disks; inboard at rear
Front Suspension:	Independent unequal A-arm w/torsion bars
Rear Suspension:	Independent w/transverse links, coil springs
Steering Type:	Rack and pinion
Turns (lock to lock):	2.6
Turning Circle (feet):	37.0

Performance

0–30 mph (seconds):	2.9
0–60 mph (seconds):	7.4
0–100 mph (seconds):	19.0
Standing 1/4 Mile (seconds):	16.7
Top Speed (mph):	150 (mfr. estimate)
Data Source:	*Road & Track*

Series I 3.8 Coupe

Number of Units Produced	7,669

Dimensions

Overall Length (inches):	175.0
Wheelbase (inches):	96.0
Width (inches):	65.2
Height (inches):	48.1
Track (inches):	50.0
Curb Weight (pounds):	2,900

Engine

Number of Cylinders:	6
Layout:	Inline; DOHC
Construction:	Alloy head; iron block
Bore x stroke (inches):	3.43x4.17
Displacement (cc/inches):	3781/230.6
Compression Ratio:	9.0/1
Horsepower Rating @ rpm	265 @ 5500
Torque Rating @ rpm (lb-ft):	260 @ 4000
Intake/Carburetion:	Three SU sidedraft

Drivetrain

Standard Transmission:	Four-speed manual (non-synchro first)
Optional Transmission:	N/A
Standard Differential Ratio:	3.31:1

Chassis and Suspension

Frame Type:	Monocoque w/front subframe
Brake Type:	Four-wheel disks; inboard at rear
Front Suspension:	Independent unequal A-arm w/torsion bars
Rear Suspension:	Independent w/transverse links, coil springs
Steering Type:	Rack and pinion
Turns (lock to lock):	2.6
Turning Circle (feet):	37.0

Performance

0–30 mph (seconds):	2.9
0–60 mph (seconds):	7.4
0–100 mph (seconds):	19.0
Standing 1/4 Mile (seconds):	15.6
Top Speed (mph):	150 (Jaguar estimate)
Data Source:	*Road & Track*

Series I 4.2 Roadster

Number of Units Produced   9,548

Dimensions
Overall Length (inches):	175.0
Wheelbase (inches):	96.0
Width (inches):	65.2
Height (inches):	48.1
Track (inches):	50.0

Engine
Number of Cylinders:	6
Layout:	Inline; DOHC
Construction:	Alloy head; iron block
Bore x Stroke (inches):	3.63x4.17
Displacement (cc/inches):	4235/258.4
Compression Ratio:	9.0/1
Horsepower Rating @ rpm	265 @ 5400
Torque Rating @ rpm (lb-ft):	283 @ 4000
Intake/Carburetion:	Three SU sidedraft

Drivetrain
Standard Transmission:	Four-speed manual
Optional Transmission:	N/A
Standard Differential Ratio:	3.07:1

Chassis and Suspension
Frame Type:	Monocoque w/front subframe
Brake Type:	Four-wheel disks; inboard at rear
Front Suspension:	Independent unequal A-arm w/torsion bars
Rear Suspension:	Independent w/transverse links, coil springs
Steering Type:	Rack and pinion
Turns (lock to lock):	2.6
Turning Circle (feet):	37.0

Performance
0–30 mph (seconds):	N/A
0–60 mph (seconds):	7.4
0–100 mph (seconds):	N/A
Standing 1/4 Mile (seconds):	14.7
Top Speed (mph):	149
Data Source:	*Classic & Sportscar*

Series I 4.2 Coupe

Number of Units Produced   7,770

Dimensions
Overall Length (inches):	175.0
Wheelbase (inches):	96.0
Width (inches):	65.2
Height (inches):	48.1
Track (inches):	50.0
Curb Weight (pounds):	2,892

Engine
Number of Cylinders:	6
Layout:	Inline; DOHC
Construction:	Alloy head; iron block
Bore x Stroke (inches):	3.63x4.17
Displacement (cc/inches):	4235/258.4
Compression Ratio:	9.0:1
Horsepower Rating @ rpm	265 @ 5400
Torque Rating @ rpm (lb-ft):	283 @ 4000
Intake/Carburetion:	Three SU sidedraft

Drivetrain
Standard Transmission:	Four-speed manual
Optional Transmission:	N/A
Standard Differential Ratio	3.07:1

Chassis and Suspension
Frame Type:	Monocoque w/front subframe
Brake type:	Four-wheel disks; inboard at rear
Front Suspension:	Independent unequal A-arm w/ torsion bars
Rear Suspension:	Independent w/transverse links, coil springs
Steering Type:	Rack and pinion
Turns (lock to lock):	2.6
Turning Circle (feet):	37.0

Performance
0–30 mph (seconds):	3.0
0–60 mph (seconds):	7.6
0–100 mph (seconds):	17.5
Standing 1/4 Mile (seconds):	15.1
Top Speed (mph):	153
Data Source:	*Autocar* (European model)

Series I 4.2 2 + 2

Number of Units Produced   5,598

Dimensions
Overall Length (inches):	184.3
Wheelbase (inches):	105.0
Width (inches):	65.2
Height (inches):	50.1
Track (inches):	50.0
Curb Weight (pounds):	3,090

Engine
Number of Cylinders:	6
Layout:	Inline; DOHC
Construction:	Alloy head; iron block
Bore x Stroke (inches):	3.63x4.17
Displacement (cc/inches):	4235/258.4
Compression Ratio:	9.0:1
Horsepower Rating @ rpm	265 @ 5400
Torque Rating @ rpm (lb-ft):	283 @ 4000
Intake/Carburetion:	Three SU sidedraft

Drivetrain
Standard Transmission:	Four-speed manual
Optional Transmission:	Three-speed automatic (Borg Warner)
Standard Differential Ratio:	3.07:1

Chassis and Suspension

Frame Type:	Monocoque w/front subframe
Brake Type:	Four-wheel disks; inboard at rear
Front Suspension:	Independent unequal A-arm w/ torsion bars
Rear Suspension:	Independent w/transverse links, coil springs
Steering Type:	Rack and pinion
Turns (lock to lock):	2.6
Turning Circle (feet):	41.0

Performance

0–30 mph (seconds):	3.4
0–60 mph (seconds):	8.3
0–100 mph (seconds):	22.5
Standing 1/4 Mile (seconds):	16.7
Top Speed (mph):	N/A
Data Source:	*Road & Track*

Series II 4.2 Roadster

Number of Units Produced   8,627

Dimensions

Overall Length (inches):	175.3
Wheelbase (inches):	96.0
Width (inches):	65.2
Height (inches):	48.1
Track (inches):	50.0
Curb Weight (pounds):	2,750

Engine

Number of Cylinders:	6
Layout:	Inline; DOHC
Construction:	Alloy head; iron block
Bore x Stroke (inches):	3.63x4.17
Displacement (cc/inches):	4235/258.4
Compression Ratio:	9.0:1
Horsepower Rating @ rpm	246 @ 5500
Torque Rating @ rpm (lb-ft):	263 @ 4000
Intake/Carburetion:	Two Zenith-Stromberg sidedraft

Drivetrain

Standard Transmission:	Four-speed manual
Optional Transmission:	N/A
Standard Differential Ratio:	3.07:1

Chassis and Suspension

Frame Type:	Monocoque w/front subframe
Brake Type:	Four-wheel disks; inboard at rear
Front Suspension:	Independent unequal A-arm w/torsion bars
Rear Suspension:	Independent w/transverse links, coil springs
Steering Type:	Rack and pinion
Turns (lock to lock):	2.8
Turning Circle (feet):	39.8

Performance

0–30 mph (seconds):	2.0
0–60 mph (seconds):	6.7
0–100 mph (seconds):	19.0
Standing 1/4 Mile (seconds):	15.3
Top Speed (mph):	119 (estimated)
Data Source:	*Car and Driver*

Series II 4.2 Coupe

Number of Units Produced   4,855

Dimensions

Overall Length (inches):	175.3
Wheelbase (inches):	96.0
Width (inches):	65.2
Height (inches):	48.1
Track (inches):	50.0
Curb Weight (pounds):	3,018

Engine

Number of Cylinders:	6
Layout:	Inline; DOHC
Construction:	Alloy head; iron block
Bore x Stroke (inches):	3.63x4.17
Displacement (cc/inches):	4,235/258.4
Compression Ratio:	9.0:1
Horsepower Rating @ rpm	246 @ 5500
Torque Rating @ rpm (lb-ft):	263 @ 4000
Intake/Carburetion:	Two Zenith-Stromberg sidedraft

Drivetrain

Standard Transmission:	Four-speed manual
Optional Transmission:	N/A
Standard Differential Ratio:	3.07:1

Chassis and Suspension

Frame Type:	Monocoque w/front subframe
Brake Type:	Four-wheel disks; inboard at rear
Front Suspension:	Independent unequal A-arm w/torsion bars
Rear Suspension:	Independent w/transverse links, coil springs
Steering Type:	Rack and pinion
Turns (lock to lock):	2.8
Turning Circle (feet):	37.0

Performance

0–30mph (seconds):	3.3
0–60mph (seconds):	8.0
0–100mph (seconds):	21.7
Standing 1/4 Mile (seconds):	15.7
Top Speed (mph):	119
Data Source:	*Road & Track*

Series II 4.2 2+2

Number of Units Produced   5,326

Dimensions

Overall Length (inches):	184.3
Wheelbase (inches):	105.0
Width (inches):	65.2
Height (inches):	50.1
Track (inches):	50.0
Curb Weight (pounds):	3,090

Engine

# of Cylinders:	6
Layout:	Inline; DOHC
Construction:	Alloy head; iron block
Bore x Stroke (inches):	3.63x4.17
Displacement (cc/inches):	4235/258.4

Compression Ratio: 9.0/1
Horsepower Rating @ RPM   246 @ 5500
Torque Rating @ RPM (lb-f.):   263 @ 4000
Intake/Carburetion: 2 Zenith-Stromberg sidedraft

Drivetrain
Standard Transmission: Four-speed manual
Optional Transmission: Three-speed automatic (Borg Warner)
Standard Differential Ratio: 3.07.1

Chassis and Suspension
Frame Type: Monocoque w/ front subframe
Brake Type: Four-wheel disks; inboard at rear
Front Suspension: Independent unequal A-arm w/ torsion bars
Rear Suspension: Independent w/ transverse links, coil springs
Steering Type: Rack and pinion
Turns (lock to lock):   2.8
Turning Circle (feet):   41.0

Performance
0 - 30mph (seconds):   N/A
0 - 60mph (seconds):   8.9
0 - 100mph (seconds):   N/A
Standing 1/4 Mile (seconds):   16.4
Top Speed (mph):   136
Data Source: *Classic & Sportscar* (auto trans)

Series III 5.3 V-12 Roadster

Number of Units Produced   7,990

Dimensions
Overall Length (inches):   184.4
Wheelbase (inches):   105.0
Width (inches):   66.1
Height (inches):   48.1
Track, F/R (inches):   54.4/53.4
Curb Weight (pounds):   3,380

Engine
of Cylinders: 12
Layout: 60 degree V; SOHC heads
Construction: Alloy block and heads
Bore x Stroke (inches):   3.54 x 2.76
Displacement (cc/inches):   5343/326
Compression Ratio: 9.0:1
Horsepower Rating @ RPM (SAE net)   250 @ 6000
Torque Rating @ RPM (lb-ft):   288 @ 3500
Intake/Carburetion: 4 Zenith-Stromberg sidedraft 2V

Drivetrain
Standard Transmission: Four-speed manual
Optional Transmission: Three-speed automatic (Borg Warner)
Standard Differential Ratio: 3.54

Chassis and Suspension
Frame Type: Monocoque w/ front subframe
Brake Type: Four-wheel disks; inboard at rear
Front Suspension: Independent unequal A-arm w/ torsion bars
Rear Suspension: Independent w/ transverse links, coil springs
Steering Type: Rack and pinion; power assisted
Turns (lock to lock):   3.5
Turning Circle (feet):   36.3

Performance
0 - 30mph (seconds):   3.3
0 - 60mph (seconds):   7.4
0 - 100mph (seconds):   18.5
Standing 1/4 Mile (seconds):   15.4
Top Speed (mph):   135
Data Source: *Road & Track;* 1972 Model

Series III 5.3 V-12 2+2

Number of Units Produced   7,297

Dimensions
Overall Length (inches):   184.5
Wheelbase (inches):   105.0
Width (inches):   66.0
Height (inches):   48.9
Track, F/R (inches):   54.4/53.4
Curb Weight (pounds):   3,361

Engine
of Cylinders: 12
Layout: 60 degree V; SOHC heads
Construction: Alloy block and heads
Bore x Stroke (inches):   3.54x2.76
Displacement (cc/inches):   5343/326
Compression Ratio: 9.0:1
Horsepower Rating @ RPM: 250 @ 6000
Torque Rating @ RPM (lb-ft):   288 @ 3500
Intake/Carburetion: 4 Zenith-Stromberg sidedraft 2V

Drivetrain
Standard Transmission: Four-speed manual
Optional Transmission: Three-speed automatic (Borg Warner)
Standard Differential Ratio: 3.54

Chassis and Suspension
Frame Type: Monocoque w/front subframe
Brake Type: Four-wheel disks; inboard at rear
Front Suspension: Independent unequal A-arm w/torsion bars
Rear Suspension: Independent w/transverse links, coil springs
Steering Type: Rack and pinion; power assisted
Turns (lock to lock):   3.5
Turning Circle (feet):   36.3

Performance
0 - 30mph (seconds):   2.6
0 - 60mph (seconds):   6.5
0 - 100mph (seconds):   15.8
Standing 1/4 Mile (seconds):   14.4
Top Speed (mph):   145
Data Source: *Autosport;* 1971 European model

Total Units Produced, 1961 - 1974:   72,520

Notes to Specifications

All specifications given are for U.S. models, unless otherwise noted.

A compression ratio of 8.00:1 was optional on six-cylinder E-Types at various times throughout production, and/or in various markets.

Optional rear axle ratios include: 2.93, 3.07, 3.31, 3.54, 3.77, and 4.09, again depending upon model year, equipment ordered, and country of original sale/homologation.

Production figures include left-hand and right-hand-drive models.

Index